DIARY OF A DELINQUENT EPISODE

DIARY OF A DELINQUENT EPISODE

JANE SPARROW
A residential social worker

ROUTLEDGE & KEGAN PAUL
London, Henley and Boston

First published in 1976
by Routledge & Kegan Paul Ltd
76 Carter Lane,
London EC4V 5EL,
Reading Road,
Henley-on-Thames,
Oxon RG9 1EN and
9 Park Street,
Boston, Mass. 02108, USA
Manuscript typed by Jennifer R. Poole
Printed and bound in Great Britain
by Unwin Brothers Limited,
The Gresham Press, Old Woking, Surrey
A member of the Staples Printing Group
© Jane Sparrow 1976

ISBN 0 7100 8340 8

CONTENTS

FOREWORD

It seems fitting that I should contribute a preface to Jane
Sparrow's book, because her residential experience is similar to
mine. But it is equally appropriate that my introduction should be
brief, because her diary speaks for itself - more convincingly
perhaps than a textbook or a research monograph on 'daily experience
in residential life' for children and their care-givers.

Students on residential social work courses are generally
encouraged by their tutors to keep a diary during practical
placements in order to record 'happenings' and interactions between
themselves and other parties involved in the daily caring
situation - with the idea that periodic discussion of such material
may provide a helpful learning opportunity. Naturally, students
vary as to whether they prefer to talk or write about their work,
and the effectiveness of either alternative will be determined
partly by the quality of response they receive from the listener or
reader. Jane Sparrow's record is slightly different in that she
needed to write privately for herself alone as she had few safe
outlets available for shared communication otherwise.

When one is caught up in a peculiarly stressful, isolated
situation, it is easy to believe one's experience is wholly unique;
that it will not ring bells for other residential workers elsewhere
or for parent-figures of younger children in care, or for body-
guards of dependent adults in prison and hospital, or for
schoolteachers in ordinary day-schools. The sheer loneliness of
this one person's current position makes it seem unlikely that
anyone else has lived through anything similar. Indeed, any comfort
derived from gradually realizing that one's own experience was in
fact far from unique might be offset by the distress of recognizing
its fairly commonplace nature. Paradoxically, one person in a tight
corner will often yearn to be part of a crowd and yet wish to savour
the drama of standing alone without competition from fellow-
sufferers and without risking loss of identity through wallowing
amidst a noble army of martyrs. Perhaps then, if there is limited
satisfaction in turning to others in comparable difficulties, it is
all the more important that there should be someone available as
confidant outside the immediate pressures - someone who can
empathize (share thoughts and feelings, with an individual or with a
group of similarly-placed individuals) without being overwhelmed.

Possibly this diary illustrates an extreme example of residential
pressures. I hope so, but they are none the less typical pressures;
neither can it be argued that they are no longer true of today. In
my view the account has value now because it highlights common,
continuing problems inherent in residential living which may be less
conspicuous elsewhere but certainly remain equally real. Jane
Sparrow brings alive the conflicts surrounding discipline and
control of numerous individuals in a group setting; the tightrope
which must be walked between exercising ineffectual or excessive
control (there is an almost archetypal flavour in the two
contrasting régimes described); the temptations of fearful grown-ups
to be punitive when faced by defiant behaviour, or to seek easy
popularity by cashing in on colleagues' strictness; the painful
tensions of staff relationships, and the frustrations of trying to
communicate with external authority-figures who 'do not want to
know'. She also shows that acceptance of disturbed adolescents is
not demonstrated by denying the reality of their interpersonal
problems, nor (at the other extreme) by treating them as dangerous
animals. In particular she depicts the strain of trying to keep a
sense of perspective and purpose when isolated long-term in
threatening circumstances, and how difficult it may prove to find a
reliable outsider in a strong enough position to offer appropriate
help.
    Clearly the workers' predicament (and therefore the girls' plight
also) would have been eased had an external support-figure been
available to respond to problems expressed subjectively by staff,
and presumably to respond separately to the great pressures of the
two contrasting persons successively responsible for leadership of
the place. Residential staff, because of the very nature of their
work, tend to be anecdotal in discussion; so this book, in
illustrating the kinds of problem they would naturally wish to raise
with a reliable helper, suggests how such discussion on an
experiential level would tend to enhance the quality of shared daily
experience in a residential setting. The diary is refreshingly free
of social work jargon - evidently words such as 'ambivalent' and
'paranoid' did not feature in the writer's vocabulary, so it is all
the more convincing when she describes these states unwittingly.
Lest these preliminaries appear to augur a horrific story, let me
add now that the content is softened (or painfully sharpened,
according to one's perception) by patches of humour. But there is
nothing shocking in store unless the reader is already convinced of
the importance of respect for persons.
    There are two reasons why I have few qualms in using Jane
Sparrow's diary as a platform for expressing briefly my own ideas
here: first, because (as mentioned above) my residential experience
is closely akin to hers. Second, because we both want, in our
individual ways, to make some small contribution towards
ameliorating the pressures too often experienced by residents and
their care-givers.

Juliet Berry
University of Sheffield

AUTHOR'S NOTE

This diary falls somewhere between 'fact' and fiction. It is
written from one person's viewpoint whilst living through a
confusing, often frightening experience. Other people within the
same situation would naturally have their own individual and
different pictures. Even if they each contributed a separate
chapter of accidents from their own viewpoint, readers might still
be left uncertain as to whose exactly was the 'delinquent episode'.
As I make no pretence to objective knowledge of what is true of
other people's experience even when living alongside them (though I
may surely claim some small understanding of my own experience) and
as I am not motivated now by a spirit of sensational bean-spilling
or retribution, I do not need to cover myself against possible
repercussions of publication. However, it can be said that this
version of the diary contains no real names of people or places.
The recorded events happened a long time ago now, and need cause no
further nightmares to any of the original participants, who
co-existed at a time when there was far less expectation of overt
violence in everyday life than perhaps there is today. The diary
was first written during the final few months of my five-year period
of work in an institution for adolescent girls. Thus it cannot
accurately be termed a diary but more a summary before leaving my
first job in my late twenties. Now middle-aged, I edit the original
'diary' for publication, not using the benefits of hindsight and a
more successful subsequent career, but retaining the limited insight
possessed earlier when in the thick of events. The following pages
can therefore be regarded somewhat as fiction because of their
highly subjective nature.

Jane Sparrow

DRAMATIS PERSONAE IN TWO REGIMES

In general, the girls are introduced simply by their Christian names; members of staff are referred to by surnames or nick-names, and all the cows have names beginning with H.

Successive heads: Miss Gracey, Mrs Strang.
Successive deputies: Miss Oldham, Miss Scott, Miss Palethorpe.
Successive schoolteachers: Miss Oldham/Nan Fulborne, Miss Dorcas, Miss Palethorpe, Anna Herrison.
House-staff at various times: Miss Naylor, Miss Wass, Mrs Briggs, Tommy, Iris Baker, Miss Crandle.
Successive cooks/domestic science teachers: Miss Crandle, Alice Sykes, Miss Curtis, Miss Sidebottom.
Garden staff: Mr Marsh, helped by Bill Evans.
Farm staff: Jane Sparrow, helped successively by (Miss Dale), Iris Baker, Miss Groves, Sarah Smythe, Joyce Romanes, Paddy.
Part-time workers: Mrs Darby, Mrs Pemberton and others.
Committee members: Mrs Percy, Mr Forbes, Mrs Hotchkiss, Mr French, Mrs de Villiers and others.
Inspectors: Miss Merton, Mr Dean, Miss Florence, Miss Amos, Mr Findley.

NOTE

Occasionally, changes of tense between past, present and future may appear incongruous or puzzling, but these should make sense to the reader if he visualizes the author writing on the premises about her five years' experience during the final few months of that period - so that her diary eventually catches up with the present. Also, some people and situations continue throughout the narrative whereas others soon become past history. A third reason for any apparent incongruity is that the writer is about to change her way of life, and it is not untypical for a person to show some confusion about past, present and future in these circumstances.

CHAPTER 1

It is now 31 May 19X9, and I am due to leave Downcroft on 7
September. I dread leaving, partly because I love the work here in
so many ways and am bound up with the whole place – also because I
half expect that the prolonged pressures of these last five years
will only catch up with me after I have left, and that it may not be
easy to adapt to life outside a residential institution. So I have
decided to write this account now in order to have something
concrete to take with me, and because I want above all eventually to
understand better what has happened here – and therefore need to
remember how it felt at the time. (I shall smuggle it out of the
building bit by bit and if you, Mrs S, should happen to discover it
before it is finished, there would be no point in your taking any
action or destroying it because I should simply rewrite the whole
thing after leaving. As I am still slightly unsure whether you
basically mean well, you would be wise to keep quiet and give
yourself the benefit of the doubt – in any case, I am very sorry to
have added to your problems here, so there is no need to be too
frightened.)

When I first saw the advertisement for a rural science teacher in a
special boarding-school for 'delinquent girls', I knew this was
exactly what I wanted, though I was not aware of my ignorance about
what the job might entail. The interview was quickly arranged for
late May 19X4, and I travelled with surprising certainty to the
small country town of Glebe.
    Downcroft is a rambling old house set in a compact rectangle of
nearly twenty acres, of which fourteen acres belong to the farm and
the remainder consist of a large and fertile garden – lawns,
vegetables, flowers, green-houses, orchards. A very polite girl
opened the front door, and showed me upstairs to the Head's
sitting-room. My impression of the house included polished floors,
cream distemper and chintz curtains blowing in the wind. The Head,
Miss Gracey, was friendly and said she had taken up her own
appointment only a few weeks before – a dignified woman in early
middle age, soft-voiced, with a weathered yet cultured face and
manner. She asked one of the girls to show me round the small farm:
well designed buildings including a classroom, three fields, and

paddocks containing two dairy cows, a heifer and a calf, two sows
with litters, hens, ducks, goats, rabbits (and bees, I discovered
later).

The interviewing panel consisted of Miss Gracey and eight
committee members. We had just started when one woman exclaimed,
'My dear, I'm getting absolutely soaked!' Water was pouring over
her through a crack in the ceiling. Miss Gracey rushed out. I
thought how embarrassing if I had left a tap running upstairs. It
turned out to be a large vase of flowers blown over by the wind in
Miss Gracey's rooms overhead, and was effective in creating a less
formal atmosphere. They asked me numerous questions about the
farming aspect: was I strong enough, would I work alongside the
girls instead of merely supervising them, would I try to decrease
the vet's bills.... They continued by saying the farm was a less
important side of the job: would I enter into the whole life of the
school, was I a member of any church, was I unshockable, and what
would I do if I had to deal with two girls fighting each other? To
this last question, I replied that I was unsure but would hope to
manage if and when the situation arose, and that I supposed 'it
would depend on my personal relationship with the two girls'.

This answer was received with a short, respectful silence as
though something special had been said, and then they chorused
enthusiastically that I had 'put the whole thing in a nutshell'.
Possibly it was a crucial question because the three other
applicants later confided that they severally had prescribed pepper,
a bucket of water (offputting to a soaked committee member?) and
turning a blind eye. Ironically, nobody present may have known from
first-hand experience the sheer berserk squalor of such a
fight - certainly I was visualizing the minor quarrels of my
schooldays. (I was well qualified in rural science and education at
twenty-three years old, but otherwise had no greater understanding
of 'personal relationships' than any young layman.) Yet I was
offered the job, and accepted it gladly after asking whether they
still wanted me knowing that I was engaged to be married but would
stay for a year. Miss Gracey shook hands with me outside the room,
saying how pleased she was. I did not realize then the importance
to her of new members of staff, as most of the old stalwarts were
leaving soon after her appointment and being replaced by well-
meaning novices like myself. This is my first job. I left after
the interview without qualms and without meeting any others of the
staff and girls.

About two months later I arrived by train with my worldly
possessions - a trunk and a bicycle - to start work at the beginning
of August. Downcroft was empty as everyone had gone on an outing,
except Miss Dale who was here to greet me. She was leaving in a few
days after introducing me to the farm routine, having been managing
it temporarily. She is an attractive person, most popular with the
girls, so the changeover seemed disappointing for them. I unpacked
in the pleasant bed-sitting room allotted to me - with easy access
to the back door for nocturnal visits to the farm, but no
bookshelves. When the coach-trip returned in the evening, with
girls singing and cheering at the top of their voices - 'Two four
six eight, who do we appreci-ate?' - I suddenly felt apprehensive as
to whether I would be appreciated, though initially the girls proved
almost more welcoming than the staff.

   At supper-time I met Miss Oldham (Deputy and schoolteacher), Miss
Naylor and Miss Wass (both leaving within a few weeks) - they half-
ignored me the first few days but were conversational after that.
Timid Miss Thomas, known as Tommy, was newish and the only adult as
young as myself. Mrs Darby (a dear, like a cottage loaf) and old
Mrs Briggs (said to be a tartar to new colleagues but always nice to
me) are both local people who have built their widowed lives round
Downcroft. All these members catered for the domestic and
educational aspects inside the house. Mr Marsh and Bill Evans
(head-gardener and his assistant) have cottages on the back drive.
   After prayers in the hall, before the girls went to bed, Miss
Gracey introduced me to them while I shook hands with each one - the
last time we have performed such a civilized ceremony. Surprisingly,
as the girls were so extremely important to her, she was unable to
identify several of them, and they winced when she mistook their
names. Perhaps this was my first indication that all was not well.
Within the next day or two, I sensed an atmosphere among the staff.
The former Head, highly regarded, had resigned for higher things
about six months before, inevitably unsettling her solid team. Miss
Oldham had been Acting Head until Miss Gracey arrived but remained
reluctant to hand over the reins. No new girls were admitted during
the interim period, but numbers were building up again, so there
were twenty-two girls when I arrived and we were to increase quite
quickly to a maximum of thirty-five.
   Gradually I heard details and anecdotes of Downcroft from its
inception, so that now (five years later) I feel I have intimate
knowledge of eleven years of history and shall miss not knowing in
future. Miss Oldham was a gaunt-looking woman, tough as old boots,
but with a vulnerable smile, perhaps a bit of a sensationalist -
though no doubt we all must be that way inclined if we stay here
long. The girls seemed at ease with her in that she knew them
through and through, made no bones about their wilder side and
enjoyed them with bleak warmth - a natural disciplinarian. When I
came, the girls were still well in hand from the previous régime,
but the more experienced staff members were appalled by Miss
Gracey's new-broom tactics, seeing trouble ahead and disagreeing
openly with her.
   Miss Gracey had been translated to Downcroft through a chance
meeting with an influential person while picking blackberries. One
can see how it happened, as she tends to drop everything in order to
go and pick wild flowers or watch the sunset, which was delightful
unless colleagues assumed she was still on duty. She is the sort of
person required for such headships in theory, of whom there are too
few, although it might have been advisable for her to serve an
apprenticeship first. Her epitaph here is 'Of course, Miss Gracey
was a lady' - an absent-minded, artistic, idealistic lady, pig-
headed in the gentlest way. She wished to treat the girls as
'normal young adults' and to change their customary routines into
more creative ways of living. 'Do it with a good will, folk', she
would say, and her first nick-name (which deteriorated to Gracey-
balls) was Miss Good-will. She seemed an odd mixture: a lover of
mankind but too talkative to listen, highly courageous but unable to
face hard facts, quite unsparing of herself but self-centred, a
muddled perfectionist, good company and yet sometimes irritating.

She rarely met one's eyes, which may have been a way of protecting
herself. Looking back, I think she was a saint. She might have
thrived here given quarter of a chance. She was reputed to have a
hot temper, but we never saw her lose it even under constant,
extreme provocation. We took much for granted, such as freedom of
speech and action, and the fact that she avoided discussing one
member of staff with another. She professed willingness to discuss
her methods with anybody but few of us took up the offer. I agreed
with her in theory but was too green to argue about practice.

It was impressive to see how the various departments dovetailed:
house, kitchen, laundry, schoolroom, farm, garden. The day was
divided into three sessions - morning, afternoon and evening. We
were supposed to work two sessions a day, but when it emerged that I
did not know this after a week, Miss Oldham informed Miss Gracey
with gleeful reproach. At first we spent almost as many hours in
recreation with the girls as in planned work and supervision duties.
It is a long day, from before 7 a.m. until 9.30 p.m. or later. But
in these early weeks things moved at a relaxed tempo in a discreetly
ordered way. One evening, Miss Gracey suggested a fancy dress
parade for which we lent girls our clothes on request. While I was
robing one girl she pointed to my ring and said, 'Well, Miss
Sparrow, I don't blame you for catching your man.' I laughed, and
another girl said, 'Don't dare speak to Miss Sparrow like that, she
ain't like us!' The girls (aged 14-17 years old) were easy to talk
with - easier than ordinary schoolchildren in some ways, and
apparently in too much need of our affection to bait us
deliberately.

After another prolonged evening's entertainment, some of us felt
hungry around midnight and cooked bacon and eggs for ourselves,
which seems extraordinary now. Also, at a sherry party when two of
the stalwarts were leaving, I talked more with Mr Marsh and Bill
Evans. I like Bill very much - a wiry little man who knows every
stick and stone of the place. He is one of the few with whom I'm on
Christian-name terms - after a year he said, 'I've wintered you and
I've summered you, so what is your first name?' His immediate boss,
Mr Marsh, is a long-winded but interesting talker, a highly skilled
gardener. On this particular evening he buttonholed me, rather
upset over having read some official document which implied that
male staff should be selected for their lack of sex appeal. It took
time for me to become on easy terms with these men as I am in charge
of the farm and they of the garden, yet they know I am better
qualified on paper without having had their thirty or forty years of
moil and toil. They offer me advice but seem inept or even alarmed
in handling livestock so I rarely turn to them for superior physical
strength. (Later I found a friend in Mr Laycock, a nearby small-
holder, who comes occasionally on request.)

Initially there were only four girls on the farm: Yvonne - a
sophisticated, muscular, politely hostile girl who never really took
to me and had nearly 'done her time'; Cynthia, said to be the most
difficult - gauche and loud-mouthed, endearing though absurdly quick
to take offence, skilled in making insulting remarks a fraction out
of earshot; little Ena, adenoidal, noisy and also touchy - a
'recall' for whom I found new employment after a month, on a poultry
farm far away (she has stayed there ever since, writing regularly

although she is barely literate, and I am to be godmother to her
coming baby now); and Patsy, the senior and most enthusiastic
worker, gifted with animals, on record as having no fewer than
twenty-one siblings in such a primitive environment that she did not
know the difference between a bra and a suspender belt on arrival
here, but who can be regarded as one of Nature's gentlewomen in
being as good as unrefined gold. She was helpful from the start,
but the others did not think much of me until I killed a cockerel
quicker than they had seen before (instantaneously) and set a hen's
broken leg. This hen received so much cosseting that she
transferred her allegiance to us and refused to rejoin her sisters
when her leg was better.

Miss Gracey liked the staff to manage their own departments
independently and to keep their own discipline, though we were able
to refer to her if necessary. I had to be firm to start with, but
ever since a basis was established it has been possible to let
things happen naturally for the most part (except with extra classes
from other departments when the school became out of hand). It is
comparatively easy on the farm because they enjoy it and there is
always a range of real work available; also the farm is situated at
a nice little distance from tensions in the house. But I think one
can only keep order effectively in one's own way. Nowadays we are
all supposed to use the same way and are almost encouraged to shout
and bluster but I never(?) shout in the house. As the girls are
more blatantly experienced in rudeness than most of the staff, I
find politeness the best way of preventing the upward spiral of a
tiff, though of course one's own 'manners' go haywire occasionally.
We could hardly have had a greater contrast of disciplinary methods
under the two Heads in my time here, but on the farm the atmosphere
has stayed fairly relaxed throughout.

In fact initially I found the animals rather more delinquent than
the girls, although it seems there is some subtle link between the
two in that girls tend to spark off excitement amongst animals and
my steadiness with the latter can have a calming effect on the
girls. These animals are unlike ordinary farm stock in having grown
up in a hotbed of conflicting emotions which goes to their heads
sometimes, but I guard them partially from the sort of rowdyism in
which they are liable to become involved (though I'm sorry to say
that when girls, staff and animals play up simultaneously it is the
latter who tend to bear the brunt of my exasperation). Animals are
sometimes thought to have extra-sensory perception of hard weather
ahead, so although my early weeks at Downcroft were outstandingly
peaceful, one or two incidents possibly foretold storms brewing
while current tensions continued almost unnoticed by me.

One vague omen was my first approach to the bees. There seemed
to be a comprehensive range of dusty bee-keeping equipment so I soon
felt obliged to summon up my scanty knowledge and inspect whether
the bees were all right. The girls and I sallied forth tightly
buttoned and veiled, too earnest to notice our strange appearance,
with our smoker emitting a cloud of false security, and I began to
dismantle the hive, making the required leisurely hypnotic
movements. The bees were wild – I was stung several times within
seconds, and put everything back without a word and with as much
speed as I dared. In some rural areas there is an old custom of

'telling the bees' of a death in the family - however, one would not
have felt confident in telling these bees anything, except to b.
off, which is exactly what they did later without being asked, so
when they absconded in a swarm I made little effort to find them.

     Another early, surprising incident was a sudden announcement from
the farm-girls that it was high time for a rat hunt: 'We have them
every so often to keep down the rats.' Before I could utter, they
were armed with pitchforks and rushed off with bloodthirsty squeals
to prod wildly in piles of hay and straw, causing danger to
themselves let alone to any wretched rat they might have flushed
out. I was sickened and put an immediate stop to this sport
although the girls were resentful over having their fun frustrated.
Our goats also proved a minor problem, getting into everything
- full of vulgar curiosity except, oddly enough, about sex. There
were few eligible billy-goats and we drove round two counties for
two years without managing to interest our nannies in breeding.
Gradually, as the farm extended in scope, I concentrated on building
up realistic numbers of cows, pigs and poultry, which seems better
preparation for later employment of my farm-girls in the outside
world. It also took two years to clean the arable land of weeds and
increase productivity. (I've just received a testimonial from the
committee chairman in which the most pleasing comment is that I
always 'kept the land in good heart', though this recommendation is
of doubtful future value as there may not be so much as a windowbox
where I'm going next.)

     I may be painting too rosy a picture of my efficiency. Having
been introduced to the farm in a casual though kindly way, and being
unbusinesslike myself then, I made my own plans for several months
without knowing of the existence of a farm and garden sub-committee
and a farms inspector, not to mention an education inspector and a
domestic inspector interested in the cheapness of my farm-produce
for the school's consumption (not TB) and a health inspector
concerned with its purity and the girls' physical labours. Much
later, as their separate suggestions sometimes conflicted, it proved
impossible to satisfy everybody. On a lower plane, I must have
irritated Mr Marsh by careless borrowing of garden tools as much as
Miss Gracey disturbed him by picking his flowers without permission.

     On first coming here I felt, maybe without quite realizing and
not altogether unpleasantly, divorced from the outside world and
from the past. This may have been partly why I suddenly and quite
unexpectedly decided to break off my engagement in mid-September
- probably a right decision though it felt miserable at the time and
it would have been better not to invest all my eggs in the Downcroft
basket from then on. I told the staff the plain fact without
elaborating, and all but two of them replied by describing their own
long past romances. But Miss Oldham took it upon herself to inform
the committee chairman (dead now) - a dear little elderly lady who
immediately came to sympathize. She extracted me from the field
where I was lifting potatoes with the girls, and walked me round the
grounds arm-in-arm in a cold wind, saying she was sure it was all
for the best and offering me open hospitality at her home. I was
mainly conscious of her smart sleeve within my earth-caked arm and
having no handkerchief handy. (Some of the committee seem even now
to keep an unusual concern for my welfare - for instance, though I

am never present at their meetings, they tend to make decisions
about the farm with a proviso 'so long as Miss Sparrow is not upset
about it'.)

This for me marked the end of the beginning here, and the end of
that summer. It had been a good summer, with the main pleasure
being our shared work together on the farm, and this has continued
over the five years.

CHAPTER 2

By late September only two violent events stand out, widely spaced
among calm days, before we began to lose whatever degree of harmony
previously existed. One was a bad fight between two girls, not
witnessed by me as it happened in the house during morning work.
Miss Oldham described how the attacker had been so consumed with
rage that she was cross-eyed for several hours afterwards. The
second event happened one evening when Miss Naylor, Number 3 on the
staff, had been left in charge - normally a thoroughly reliable,
experienced person except that she may have been anticipating
trouble under the new régime. It started in a small way through her
arguing with a large girl called Vanessa, who ran out of the house
and up the road. Six girls ran after her to bring her back. I
drove Miss Naylor after them in the school van and we brought them
all back. Then Vanessa fought against going into the detention
room - like a cell, with heavily barred window and door, bare except
for a plank bed and countless messages scratched on its walls
- until now a place just mysteriously known of to me as an empty
threat. I was amazed to see the girls turn into a kicking,
screaming mob surrounding Vanessa. Miss Naylor told me to ring the
police, which I did, thinking it normal procedure and never before
having witnessed such a scene. The girls threw Vanessa into
detention and then quietened down. When the police came it was all
over. Four girls were slightly hurt so the doctor was also called
in.

Soon after, Miss Gracey returned, went straight in to Vanessa and
talked quietly with her. She found it hard to forgive Miss Naylor,
who was due to leave in a day or two, for involving the police. I
was abashed, and found it hard to visualize Vanessa coming back into
circulation again, but of course she did - I have only slowly
learned that such events happen and that life does very soon
continue as before. However, next day, after much thought, Miss
Gracey caned Vanessa - which seemed quite out of character though
she felt there was sufficient dignity in that she somehow obtained
Vanessa's agreement beforehand. It may literally have been a case
of 'this hurts me more than it hurts you', because Miss Gracey was
said to have vomited afterwards. I have never seen a cane or
anybody being caned - there are definite rules about its use here,

but Miss Gracey did not resort to it again although she debated with
herself and me on one subsequent occasion. I can still hardly
believe it happened even once, especially as our present Head does
not allow herself her official right to cane, perhaps fearing it
could become a semi-lethal weapon in her hands.

I do not know whether Miss Gracey thought about Vanessa's record
beforehand. She had been adopted by well-to-do people who were said
to spoil her at first. When she became difficult they took her to
more than one psychiatrist for advice - one said she needed more
love and another advised a good spanking. They varied their tactics
and on more than one occasion tied her to her bed and beat her
almost unconscious. Vanessa was committed here partly because she
stole to 'buy friendship' from her schoolfellows. She had a
beautiful face with a grossly fat body, was extremely moody with
great respect for material wealth. Later on here she was at the
centre of widespread, interchangeable homosexual relationships. She
was always muddled about 'friendship' - in the end it was this which
caused both her own and the school's decline.

By early October the exodus of stalwarts was complete and their
replacements were beginning to arrive. Before now we had occasional
leisurely staff-meetings during working hours when the girls could
safely be left to their own devices - meetings in which Miss Gracey
was pleasantly vague, Miss Naylor kept saying 'I'm awfully sorry,
but...', and Miss Oldham sat keeping her own countenance (as Mrs
Briggs would say). When Miss Gracey was briefly away on leave, Miss
Oldham took over with gusto, referring to 'my girls, my staff, my
committee'. When, in turn, Miss Oldham was briefly away, Miss
Gracey had laryngitis and asked me to 'be her voice' - a little
awkward as my words are different and fewer. Ten new girls arrived
in quick succession, forming a group of 'juniors' who attended
classes in a body mostly composed of big individual bodies - some of
them arriving straight from Court with corners quite unrubbed from
any preliminary classification. Miss Gracey accepted all comers,
either on principle or through not knowing she could have some say
in choosing and timing admissions.

Our three new members of staff consisted first of Miss Crandle,
who luckily had already gained useful similar experience elsewhere,
and came to take charge of the kitchen and domestic science. I met
her at the station on arrival and picked her straight out of a small
crowd from her description of 'slim and efficient-looking'. Nan
Fulborne in a flowing cloak came to develop the teaching of art,
music and games - an enjoyable colleague who brought a touch of
flamboyance to the staff-room and neighbourhood before she left to
marry a year later. And Iris Baker came to organize housework and
to be my part-time farm assistant, having trained in rural domestic
economy - superficially seeming slightly prim but with a dry sense
of humour and a love of jaunts. We all tend to use each others'
surnames as though it would be unseemly for the girls to know we
have Christian names, unless our surnames lend themselves to nick-
names. For instance, I am usually called 'Sparrow' or 'Birdy',
possibly looking somewhat bird-like since losing the equivalent of a
fledgling's puppyfat. Anyway we settled down nicely together as a
new team.

Now that I was freer with having a farm relief assistant (who,

bless her, was better with bees than I, though this did not stop
them departing later in a swarm), I took a large share of driving
the school van - mostly to railway stations, hospitals and clinics,
police-stations, taking girls for interviews for jobs and visiting
them on aftercare. Often I chauffered Miss Oldham, say if we were
retrieving a truculent girl from a failed job, and sometimes we
drove through the night. She had a habit of lurching forward
whenever I changed gear, especially on emergency trips, not compli-
mentary to my driving, but apparently she did it to share the work
of driving. In contrast, Miss Gracey tended to sleep instead of
map-reading, or would disappear to breathe Nature, leaving me in the
van with potential runaways. It was considered an honour to drive
the school van and I developed a taste for driving far and fast.
    The main autumnal milestone was the quick arrival of these ten
new girls with a few resentful recalls and one or two 'transfers'
who had proved uncontainable elsewhere. The school was suddenly
full and I had a larger group of farm-girls from now on. By now
many girls were individually awkward from time to time, but they did
not synchronize much until after Christmas. There were occasional
fights, a few tussles with staff and some mild absconding without
anyone going far before we found them. The most difficult aspect
was that individual girls began to refuse point-blank to do as they
were asked - to get out of bed, to work, to go outside or inside,
etc. - and it could take as long as half an hour to persuade them.
It is vaguely nerve-racking to be constantly making routine
requests, never quite knowing whether girls will comply easily or
jib. We took any amount of trouble to coax and persuade - there was
certainly not 'free discipline' as is thought now to have been the
case then.
    I well remember my shock the first time I ran out of words with a
stony-faced recall who refused to come and take her turn to wash up
with three others. I automatically took her arm, not to force her
but just because there was nothing more to say. She reacted like
lightening: 'Take your filthy hands off me.' This is a set phrase,
which I had not heard before, and I took it at face-value after
staring briefly in bewilderment. I think I replied that I would go
and start the washing-up and would have clean hands by the time she
joined me, which she soon did surreptitiously. The same girl
diddled me into confessing my age by feigning sympathy over whether
I was 'too young for this work' - I reassured her (and myself) that
one was no longer hampered by youthfulness at the good age of
twenty-three, and then realized my age would be broadcast and would
be considered unsuitable information by some colleagues.
    In fact I was quite frequently taken for a girl during my first
year, partly because my farm clothes are very like those worn by
farm and garden girls (but can be smartened indoors by a rapid
change of boots and jacket). One new girl confided later that she
had considered asking me to be her best friend on arrival, a short-
sighted committee member chased me in her car in broad daylight, a
party of visiting magistrates enquired, 'What's that little one in
for?' and I was caught four times by the police after dark. The
police are not supposed to manhandle the girls but seem to make the
most of actually catching them as an initial deterrant. Once they
were extremely rough, having pounced without warning in pitch

darkness while I was walking down the drive in my free time.
Startled, I said something scathing in defence (though not to the
extent of saying 'Take your filthy hands off me') and Sergeant Bibby
seems to regard me as a bit of a spitfire since then.

Miss Gracey sometimes went off duty without saying so. Iris
Baker and I happened to see her walking off under a red umbrella one
Saturday to a Musical Afternoon at the local grammar school. 'Good
thing we saw her go,' said Iris, 'now we know we're in charge.' She
took a single girl, disappointed about home-leave, out for a cream
tea miles away, leaving a very lean staff. In November a new girl,
Dawn, arrived by car with two probation officers who had had a
hair-raising long journey with her, so on arrival they left us to
cope. We were not expecting her and did not know that Head and
Deputy were out. Dawn, very tough and weighing over twelve stone,
refused to come indoors. The secretary and I went out and talked to
her, mutely clinging to the car, and after a longish time she burst
into tears and came in quietly.

But Miss Gracey did know the art of gracious living. For a few
months it was a happy mixture of work and play, with a glass-of-
sherry-before-Sunday-lunch touch, pleasant to me after years of
being a poor student. We often went to her sitting-room after
9.30 p.m., listening to music and sipping China tea with lemon. She
had a special record which she seemed to play when troubled in
spirit - a hauntingly sad, beautiful melody, not well known so I
have never heard it since and would not wish to now - gradually one
heard it more and more, crying out gently from her room when she was
alone there at night. She produced a Nativity play for Christmas.
I can hear the noise of those long-drawn-out rehearsals now. There
was a flock of 'sheep' who were supposed to bleat briefly off-stage.
They all bleated interminably while Miss Gracey raised her voice to
coach the principal actors. I sat uneasily in the staff-room,
wishing they were real sheep whom I could soon have guided further
afield to safely graze.

We put great effort into Christmas 19X4 and I enjoyed the
preparations more than anything. The night before Christmas Eve we
all gathered to fill the girls' stockings with much hilarity until
after 1 a.m. On Christmas Eve I was extra busy with the girls,
finishing poultry trussing. In the evening, Miss Gracey started to
make a crib. At 11 p.m. I found Nan Fulborne swearing in the art
room while she designed the crib backcloth. Miss Crandle was busy
cooking all night without ever going to bed. Miss Gracey and I took
the communicants to a midnight service, and returned arm-in-arm with
affectionate girls, but found trouble back at home over a dormitory
'feast' and I got to bed after 2 a.m. At 3.30 a.m. Miss Gracey had
nearly finished the crib and wandered into my bedroom to ask if I
had any wooden animals for it. I said 'Help yourself' and went back
to sleep. At 6 a.m. Iris Baker and I rose to do pre-breakfast farm
duty by ourselves so as to give our girls a holiday treat - best bit
of the day for us.

At 7.30 a.m. on Christmas morning we came in and joined the whole
school, unwashed in their nighties, while they opened their
stockings and presents. Miss Gracey began fooling about (she cannot
have felt a bit like it), expecting me to join in. Forced jollity
embarrasses me. Afterwards it appeared the girls thought she was

drunk - poor woman to be so misjudged! Then the staff cleared up a mountain of paper and string, and we all trooped in to breakfast together. I had neither time nor energy to open my own parcels that day. Twice we withdrew for a glass of sherry but were unable to finish it. Things grew steadily worse as the day wore on - we could not make it 'happy' because the girls were wild. Actually nothing makes it a happy day for the girls unless they are remembered by their families - some do not even receive a card. Turkey dinner in the evening was hectic. There were one or two bad cases of hysteria then and next day. Gladys chanted 'I want me mum, I want me mum' for what seemed like hours. I vividly remember Iris Baker being sent for water and returning with it in her sedate manner in a small white teapot. (She and I made fools of ourselves more than once by fetching too little or too much water on such occasions - notably when we turned up like Jack and Jill with a whole bucketful having tersely been told 'Water', but the doctor only wanted a glass of water while sedating a girl in detention.) Cathy roamed about, quite mad, wearing a carnival hat inscribed 'I'm no Angel', and towards bedtime began breaking furniture.

Mistakenly we had all got unnecessarily overtired at Christmas.

CHAPTER 3

It was immediately after Christmas that the real trouble began. It lasted from 27 December until the following late autumn. It is impossible to describe those eleven months - we were deemed to have a semi-official riot at the very end but by some definitions one could say we had them several times a week, sometimes several daily. A proper riot seems to mean involvement en masse rather than small group violence. Few if any of us seriously considered leaving during this time, partly because we never visualized it continuing so long, also we seemed as committed as the girls though in a different way. It is hard to convey that we remained on fairly friendly terms with the girls throughout, and that this was only interrupted, not lost, by small or larger upheavals. Nothing would induce me to live through this again but, once in it, we had little thought of escape through resigning our posts. Also we grew close as a team - we simply could not afford to bicker among ourselves, nor did we meet enough socially to irritate each other. Our meals and sleep, even baths, were often disrupted - I lost 1½ stone in weight during the first three months, having been too plump, and have stayed at eight stone.

The worst of the absconding, though it went on all the time, was from January to June, when we suddenly pieced together the main escape route. Lorry drivers were wise to us, and one could be offered a lift within minutes from the back gate. The girls got further afield - mostly to London - and there was an aftermath of visits to the VD clinic and police statements about thefts outside. My task was usually to drive off in the van, either searching or bringing them home, which was preferable in a way to staying in the restless building. Miss Gracey was talking to Iris Baker once about the worst period of absconding - 'Let me see,' she said, 'were you with us then?' Iris said to me, 'I know I didn't do much, but it was hell waiting and trying to keep the others quiet.' Similarly, at the next meal after some horrid scene, Miss Gracey would recount it from A to Z although most of us would have been present assisting - if one or two people came late to the meal we would have to hear it all over again.

When we got absconders back, usually late or during the night, we stood in the entrance hall while plans were made, depending on their

state. I always hated that, wondering whether they would go to bed
quietly or struggle. 'Unfold your arms', they would be told, and I
would surreptitiously unfold mine - it is considered an insolent
attitude in these circles, but I find it protective. Sometimes
individuals would throw themselves into our arms weeping, and I
would hold mine gently, not altogether sympathetically, but thinking
it the most economical way of dealing with numbers as it takes at
least two people to hold a violent girl and three to move them
anywhere. A preliminary stage is to remove their boots or shoes so
they can do less damage in kicking. A less weighty member does this
while others hold her, and one bends down to their feet half-fearing
a kick in the face. Mr Marsh and Bill gave limited help partly
because they do not live in the house, also in one way they are more
vulnerable than women - threatened by a kick 'where you wouldn't
like to show your mum'. Miss Gracey disliked using the detention
room but it seemed impossible not to do so, and sometimes any of
several small lockable rooms were brought into use. Girls cannot
have anything with which they might hurt themselves (belt,
hairgrips, etc.) which often involves a second struggle in detention
while removing such objects. Often the house was kept awake by the
noise of the person screaming or singing in detention.

The problem of 'best mates' developed rapidly after Christmas
until nearly all girls were involved, apart from one or two who
could dream only of men, and one or two desperately unattractive
girls who tended to attach themselves to an established pair and
pick up any crumbs of comfort which might fall their way. The
'couples' kept changing, which caused constant unrest, jealousy and
fighting. Most of the activity went on during the night, but became
more open during the day, and was soon regarded as normal by the
girls. There was no very constructive policy to deal with it - it
was some time before we realized how far it went, and knew about the
'feelers', carrots, etc. Even when we knew, Miss Gracey could not
believe it until she had telephoned a nun in charge of a similar
school, and learned that all this is not uncommon in closed one-sex
communities. She tried very hard to talk privately with girls about
'the beauty of ordinary sexual relationships' but they remained
unconvinced. Many months later we were told by inspectors that we
had been wrong to regard it as widespread homosexual behaviour, that
probably only Vanessa was a 'real homosexual'. This to me was
neither here nor there - the main problem was the general feverish
unrest, and our being unsure how best to cope.

I dreaded mealtimes and prayers most. On waking each morning I
would reckon what meal-duties were in store that day and what chance
there was of Miss Oldham being in charge. Three of us were on duty
in the girls' dining-room - Head or Deputy, a kitchen server, and a
junior member who then supervised the washing-up (the rest eating in
the staff dining-room in slightly more comfort). Sometimes I was
just breathing Amen thankfully after Miss Oldham said Grace, when
Miss Gracey would change her mind and decide to take the meal
herself. Breakfast was usually better than dinner and supper could
be worst of all. It was often an uproar, plates flying with or
without food on them, overturned teapots and chairs, shouting and
swearing, excluded girls demonstrating outside the windows and
having food passed out to them. Often we waited for minutes for

things to quieten before the meal started. At the end of the meal,
especially if it had gone fairly well, one hoped desperately that
Miss Gracey would leave quickly without a little homily to the
girls - often on minor points of etiquette such as putting salt at
the side of one's plate instead of sprinkling it wholesale, which
seemed utterly immaterial. We stood up. 'Now, folk...', she would
begin, but rarely had chance to finish uninterrupted, and her
frequent use of 'Steady, folk' seemed to have a particularly
unfortunate effect. Our table was furthest away from the door on a
dais and one felt trapped. We left the room in order of rank with
as much dignity as we could muster, and with other ranks closing in
alarmingly quickly behind us.
      Miss Gracey's birthday in late January was most distressing. It
lasted almost exactly twenty-four hours and was particularly
agonizing because she took it for granted that the school would
enjoy her birthday with her. I returned some keys to her room late
the previous night and found her writing up her log book, unaware of
the time, laughing at herself for having a cracked lens in her
spectacles, charming and maddening. I said, 'It's just on midnight
so I'll wish you a happy birthday but then let's start it in the
morning.' Two girls absconded soon after twelve, and Miss Oldham
and I were called out to fetch them from a police-station about
3 a.m. The school rose at 7 a.m. in a nasty frame of mind, and sang
'Happy birthday dear Miss Gracey' in mocking tones before breakfast.
Morning work went quite well except that several windows were
broken. I was on dinner-duty with Miss Gracey - nerve-racking - at
the end she told them she was treating them all to the cinema that
afternoon except for seven girls who had behaved exceptionally
badly.
      I had about fifteen minutes in which to get them all ready and
supervise the washing-up. Those going out had no time to wash up,
and the seven refused. I tried to persuade Gladys, but had not time
to persevere and told her so. (She was unlike others in being
clearly deficient mentally, and she now seems to be permanently in a
colony for subnormals.) Although I was no longer requesting her
help, she continued to follow me round, agitating. I suddenly lost
my temper and told her to shut her big mouth (a phrase I have
probably never used before or since). Gladys went to complain to
Miss Gracey, who returned to me with her, saying she knew Gladys was
lying 'because, I tell her, you are a lady and would never speak in
that way'. 'I'm afraid I did.' Miss Gracey was shocked but tried
to salvage it by telling Gladys she must have been unendurable to
have caused a lady to speak thus. 'No, she was really no worse than
usual, just the last straw, I'm sorry Gladys, I shouldn't have said
that to you.'
      The cinema-goers departed, leaving Gladys unable to forgive me,
apparently only aware that she had first been insulted and then
accused falsely of lying. She became violent and Miss Oldham, Mrs
Briggs and I struggled to move her to sick bay, where she calmed
down after throwing the weighing-scale weights through the closed
windows. Meanwhile, on the way to the cinema, Cathy told Miss
Gracey conversationally that she would like to murder her. Outside
the picture-house afterwards, in a scene, Lynne told her the same
thing. Miss Oldham told me this at teatime, saying the two girls

had now joined forces, and there was a razor-blade missing. Miss
Oldham may have been dramatizing slightly, but I took her dead
seriously at the time. We decided to say nothing direct to Miss
Gracey because it was her birthday and she would not heed a warning
anyway, but to keep an eye on Cathy and Lynne ourselves to see that
Miss Gracey was not left alone with them. Two more girls absconded
at some point.

During the evening (when Miss Gracey and I were on duty together)
she asked me to stay in the common-room while she went to look for
Cathy and Lynne, who 'seem to have disappeared'. I said I would
rather not stay alone with the large group; would she mind staying
there while I went to look for the missing two. She agreed easily,
and I looked round the house with my mouth completely dry, so that I
could not have spoken had I found them. In fact they were in the
garden. We could have tried to fetch them in, but Miss Oldham said
let them go. At about 9 p.m. the police rang, and Miss Oldham and I
drove a few miles to bring Lynne and Cathy back. The police said
they 'had got it into their heads to murder the head lady', and that
they were so violent that they would transport them and put them
into detention for us — most unusual but welcome. At 11.30 p.m.
colleagues returned with the other two absconders, and it was just
on midnight when they, and the staff clothes they took with them,
were sorted out.

That was the twenty-four hours of Miss Gracey's birthday in which
she was probably the only perfectly 'ladylike' person throughout.
It may have been a turning-point for me. I became more rather than
less distressed for her, but began to feel irritated with her for
exposing herself and all Downcroft inmates to such inner and outer
turmoil. She changed her tactics at some stage and became firmer,
but it was too late for the girls and only made them dislike her
more. She was the last person to want a violent scene, yet seemed
unable to help provoking them. She would 'reason' for ages with a
girl, who was eventually bound to become rude or fidgety. If she
had not touched them when they were on the brink of losing self-
control, they could not very well have started without actually
assaulting her. The rest of us seemed to manage to by-pass physical
violence, but we were constantly involved in rescuing her — maybe
partly because she, as Head, caught ill-feeling for all of us.

One extraordinary thing was her patience. By this time she was
having migraine and occasional black-outs, but never appeared
unruffled in temper. Of course she was older than I, but under far
more pressure of ultimate responsibility. I lost my temper three
times during these months — i.e. with Downcroft people as opposed to
farm animals and police. The first time was with Gladys as already
described. The second time was when I nearly got into a fight with
Dawn, far bigger than myself, because of her obscene defiance in
speaking of Miss Gracey after a rowdy breakfast. I would have
carried on regardless, determined to win any fight, had not my farm-
girls intervened with surprising good sense. They not only stopped
it tactfully but behaved just as usual towards me afterwards though
I was unable to thank them. The third time was during lunch once in
the girls' dining-room when Miss Gracey, Mrs Darby and I were on
dinner-duty. The room was in uproar, Miss Gracey was absent-
mindedly spooning out far too much rice-pudding for me (a pudding I

loathe) and, if we could have heard, was probably rambling on about
her home town about which we knew every detail though she seemed to
know none of our birth-places. It suddenly felt unbearable, and I
shouted out, 'Oh, bugger it!' knowing it would not be heard above
the tumult. Only Mrs Darby heard, and flinched with pursed lips.
The expression on her face - implying 'Things have come to a pretty
pass' - kept me amused for the rest of the meal.

   There were hundreds of incidents, much of a muchness. 'Never a
dull moment', Miss Oldham said, but others of us yearned for
boredom. She had gradually become very attached to Miss Gracey but
still could not give up her own power, not unnaturally by now. She
told me once that Miss Gracey had given her a week to decide whether
it was wise for her to continue as headmistress - she must have said
yes when the week was up. But I think Miss Gracey would have
persevered to this day had she been allowed. Once I asked Miss
Oldham whether we might, when Miss Gracey was on leave, assemble the
whole staff, resident and part-time, and tell the girls that we
regretted their attitude to Miss Gracey and that we were solidly
with her. Miss Oldham replied that Miss Gracey 'wouldn't like
it' - she wouldn't and I didn't myself, but thought it worth trying
and that it might make Miss Oldham hand over some of her own
authority as a by-product.

   We soon did not stick to duty hours, though we were quite free to
go out. I used to sit in the staff-room, doing the 'Guardian'
crossword, straining my ears to hear the next scene starting. Tommy
in contrast had our radio on full blast to drown the girls' noise in
their common room. So there was no peace except on the farm, and
Tommy's attitude was probably saner than mine. Iris Baker and I
complained once. We had both had a bad afternoon and happened to
say so. We were sent off in Miss Gracey's car for the evening 'to
enjoy ourselves'. We sat obediently in a pub ten miles away, very
sober, as Iris (a teetotaller) sipped pineapple juice, feeling a
little guilty, and then crept back with any grounds for complaint
cut from under our feet.

   A few of the most difficult girls were transferred to other
schools from time to time, though there always seemed to be a ready
successor to trouble-makers' shoes. There is something ruthlessly
drastic about a transfer, as it happens without warning to the girl
at crack of dawn with no good-byes except to her steely escorts. We
were immensely relieved to hear that Lynne - the only girl who has
struck me as indefinably evil - was to be transferred several weeks
hence at Easter, and that we need not go out of our way to cope with
her meanwhile. Two days before she was due to go, Miss Gracey
decided to keep Lynne with us 'as she's improved so much'. The next
evening, Sunday, I was lying on the staff-room sofa, quite happy
with a book, four kittens and some apples, when I was called out to
retrieve Lynne and Vanessa with Miss Oldham. Apparently the two had
quarrelled - one ran off and the other followed, and Vanessa tried
or pretended to drown herself in the nearby river. We brought them
back dripping. It was a sunny evening, with people walking by the
river, and a small crowd gathered, one of whom telephoned later to
ask whether we knew they were lesbians. Miss Oldham said 'Nonsense'
and rang off. Lynne had been told, perhaps unwisely, how nearly she
was transferred, and became more difficult after this.

One of the cows, Harmony, had a bad accident that winter. She
somehow wedged herself into the cowshed troughs overnight, and
battered her head in panic, losing a horn and a lot of blood. We
found her at 7.20 a.m., and it took five men until mid-morning to
extricate her by breaking concrete and steel fittings. We propped
her up between straw bales with rugs and hot water bottles. The vet
gave her an injection, and thought her likely to die, although he
said there was a chance if she could be kept alive overnight. I
gave her drenches of black coffee and brandy every two hours for the
next two nights and days (fetching absconders once or twice in
between). Iris was on leave, so after the second night my farm-
girls volunteered to do the morning work by themselves while I
slept. They managed perfectly. Helping each other over events such
as Harmony is what seems to create harmony between me and the
farm-girls. It took many months for Harmony to recover – she
developed pneumonia and pleurisy, and gave birth prematurely to a
dead calf (fortunately I was there – the vet had wanted a urine
specimen, so I was sitting in wait with a jam-jar, torch and book
when she began to calve – Iris and I buried it by torchlight. Also
her skin cracked open where she had been trapped, causing terrible
wounds which I had to syringe out twice a day. She survived by
sheer will-power and I became very fond of her in the process. The
vet, Mr Laycock and I went out for a celebratory dinner when the
worst was over.
     The girls enjoyed preparing for the Young Farmers' Club County
Rally in May. Iris and I took eight of them to the Rally. We had a
really good day – they won a lot of certificates and were runners-up
for the Schools' Cup. Cynthia was so nervous before the poultry
trussing competition that I made a rash promise of a cigarette after
the event. To her amazement she won, so we sloped off triumphantly
for an illicit smoke in the van. Normally the girls smoked anything
they could beg from men, steal from us or pick up in the street. It
seemed they often smoked under the bedclothes at night.
     We had one girl just then for three months who was only actually
with us ten days because of her constant absconding. She and Val
were picked up in the Commercial Road once, and the scene was
reported in national newspapers:
     When two police-women stopped two teenage girls yesterday, all
     hell broke loose.... For eight minutes the girls struggled
     fiercely until three car-loads of policemen arrived....
     Everything seemed to happen at once. One of the girls grabbed a
     police-woman by the hair and her face hit the kerb. The other
     girl was wrestling ... in a doorway. A crowd gathered. The
     noise was terrific. The girls fought like tiger-cats....
Head and Deputy brought them back overnight, and I was left in
charge of the school, and remember holding an imaginary conversation
aloud with Miss Oldham outside the first floor dormitories in order
to let the girls think she was there! They returned just before
breakfast with the two girls, who ran off again after lunch. I had
just read the newspapers and was sent off alone to look for them,
with a fast-beating heart. Fortunately I met Bill Evans on the way.
We caught Val quite easily near the railway line but the other girl
got to London again.
     Four habitual absconders were given a week of hard labour under

constant supervision of Miss Oldham. She was exhausted at the end
of the week but the girls, having completed a fantastic amount of
work, still found enough energy to run again. At one point, I had
just come in from doing an errand in the van in my free time, and
had grabbed a glass of beer en route - so hastily that it caused
hiccups. Miss Oldham greeted me, 'I want you to stand at the bottom
of the back stairs. I've got Pat at the top, refusing to scrub the
stairs - I've filled a bath with cold water and I've told her I'll
throw buckets of water over her till she starts work. You stand
there in case she tries to escape.' 'But I've got hiccups', I said,
feeling this might introduce improper levity into a grim situation.
Miss Oldham ignored this feeble excuse, and indeed my hiccups ceased
abruptly with the shock of seeing the first bucket of water come
cascading down round the bend in the stairs. Pat started scrubbing
after the third bucket, and I was able to leave my little paddling
pool, wishing I had stayed longer in the pub.
     In June there was an official complaint from the police about the
amount of absconding. The committee chairman came to talk to the
girls about it. The single farm-girl absconder returned from the
meeting full of glee: 'It's going to be smashing here, Miss Sparrow,
we're going to have our own clothes in the evenings, and more free
time, and boy-friends and cigarettes and outings....' Apparently
the chairman opened the proceedings by asking why they ran away, and
finished by making a list of wants (none of which were granted).
     One Friday after lunch, Head and Deputy took four extra-truculent
girls to the VD clinic, leaving four of us behind to cope.
Immediately after they had gone, my farm-girls came in a body to see
me in the staff-room, wanting to know whether I regarded Cynthia or
Patsy as more senior. Cynthia had bullied the others into being on
her side. I dealt with them superficially by saying both rivals
were senior in different ways, and sent them swiftly back to their
common-room where Tommy was on after-dinner duty. Moments later,
Patsy and Cynthia began to fight - on the floor with their nails and
teeth at each others' eyes, throats and hair. Mrs Darby and Iris,
when we separated them, took Patsy into the staff-room. Cynthia
went on fighting at me, standing there without heat or support until
a girl helped me. Tommy went on using her sewing-machine throughout
and apologized afterwards that she 'couldn't let go of the gathers'!
Then I told Patsy that she or Cynthia would have to go into
detention, either would do, as they could not be on the farm
together that afternoon. Patsy volunteered, and walked up into
detention, quite docile. I sent Cynthia to the farm to hoe. Just
as she went, Mr Marsh came and gave her an irritating 'penny
lecture', and she nearly fought him. Then he told me that he had
advised Patsy that morning 'to fight it out with Cynthia', and I
told him it was a pity he had not been present to referee. At
teatime, when Miss Gracey returned, she thought I had treated Patsy
unfairly. In the evening, part of the heavy plaster ceiling in the
hall fell down, suddenly giving up the ghost, after silently
witnessing countless scenes.
     In June Mrs Darby left, though she is not lost to us, living
nearby. I must stress that things were far more difficult for most
of my colleagues, working in the main building, than for me who
could escape in the van or retreat much of each day to the farm.

Things might have been less fraught had we not felt obliged to try to stop every little bit of bad behaviour. For instance, I was cleaning out the pigs with Maggy one morning (an outrageously hysterical but often amusing girl, who had a habit of prolonged retching over the farmyard drains) and it took me about half an hour to stop her singing 'Roll me over in the clover'. At last we continued work peacefully, I began to feel happy and absent-mindedly started singing the same song – it has a catchy tune – but Maggy stopped me abruptly with shocked reproach. That is the funny thing about them – they have just as high standards for us as we have for them, but none of us quite bring it off, and one does wonder occasionally how much is trivial.

Visitors are often as much of an embarrassment to us as we are to them, though they are not always aware of what is going on under their noses, and we do for the most part keep up appearances. Frequently they are a sad disappointment. Our visiting chaplain came weekly to take a short evening service on Wednesdays, seeming so spiritual as to be not quite of this world, though I always attended, both through duty and in hope of inspiration. In a little sermon at the height of our disruptions, he explained to the girls that they must not think the next world is totally different to this world or that one can suddenly live differently when body and soul part company. Becoming more complex, he explained that they could expect to continue living the spiritual equivalent of whatever had been their major preoccupation on earth. 'For example,' he said, 'your staff look after you now, and in the next world their job will be to bring on backward souls.' From what I could see of their faces, the girls had either stopped listening or were prepared for us to continue our unenviable task throughout eternity but to me the prospect was overwhelming. I felt depressed beyond measure.

(More recently, our present Head introduced the award of a silver cup annually to the girl who has made the most progress – i.e. to the most mealy-mouthed girl. Mrs Percy, a committee member, came to make the first presentation with a speech. She said she wished to tell the girls something which had helped her all her life, which had indeed completely changed her life for the better, as she hoped it would ours when she told us this little phrase, almost a text.... By this time I was leaning forward in my chair, eager to catch the miraculous message dangled before us. After further build up, she confided the secret of gradual success, and spelt it out more than once: 'K-e-e-p o-n k-e-e-p-i-n-g o-n.' Her bathos, as opposed to the chaplain's unthinkable promise of future bliss, threatened to overwhelm me with weak giggles.)

But during the summer of 19X5, we began to question the possibility of continuing indefinitely as we were. The situation was almost beyond our strength to 'keep on keeping on'. I said to old Mrs Briggs, who has a rigid wisdom gained from lengthy experience, quite uneducated but giving a strongly corseted impression of always knowing best: 'How long shall we have to go on like this?' She replied mysteriously but comfortingly that 'They' would do something about it sooner or later.

CHAPTER 4

In late July Miss Merton, 'our' inspector, turned up after a year's absence on sick leave (during which time one or two other inspectors had visited at rare intervals) and stayed overnight. It was the first time most of us had met her, and we invested great hopes and fears in her coming.

Naturally, things were relatively quiet during her visit. The morning she came, Maggy somehow pinched some hexoestrol tablets I planned to implant for caponizing cockerels. She ate four, and confessed after retching over the yard drain for longer than usual. I rang the doctor (who could do nothing), very worried that I might have done permanent damage to Maggy's reproductive powers, and what would Miss Merton think, unless I had inadvertently started a new method of treatment. Mercifully it finished as a joke, because Maggy was quite all right, as I might have realized had I stopped to consider the biochemical implications.

The highlight of Miss Merton's visit for the staff was hearing her deal with two girls whom she discovered in a minor misdemeanour: 'I speak ONCE and ONCE ONLY' - such a contrast to Miss Gracey's long-drawn-out reasonings - and we repeated the phrase frequently to each other. The following day Miss Merton was due to leave immediately after having breakfast in bed. Miss Gracey and I took breakfast with the girls, and Cathy in a small scene, not dangerous but which left me slightly shaken, attacked her with a table knife. Towards the end of the meal I emerged from the dining room, with Cathy in one hand and the knife in the other, and coincided with Miss Merton's descent down the stairs, carrying her suitcase. Mrs Briggs came forward, shocked that such an important person should be left to carry her own case when tradition demands a polite girl in attendance. She whispered sharply to me to take the case and, as Cathy was suitably awed, I left her to her own devices and moved to Miss Merton, who was unaware of the knife incident apparently.

I carried the case out to Miss Merton's car. She told me I looked tired and advised me to 'take up a hobby'. I was unable to reply, being near tears at her sudden concern, and stood watching her drive away. That very evening I met a commercial traveller in the local hotel who became my hobby for the next few months. He carried me on into the next era here by which time it was becoming apparent that he had a girl in every port of call.

On my twenty-fourth birthday, Gladys (alone in discovering the
fact) gave me a box of peppermint creams in the morning inscribed
'with all my love', and stole my cigarettes in the evening, which
was hard to stomach as I can manage without chocolates far more
easily than without smoking. The girls show tremendous need both to
give things to us and take things from us. It was particularly
painful to Mrs Briggs to see the girls' lack of respect for the
headmistress. She longed to see them fetch and carry courteously
for the Head as they had in the old days here, and to wait on all of
us to some extent. While I admired Miss Gracey's unspoken belief
that a person in her position should behave with extra humility, I
think she might have done better to indulge the girls' great desire
to do things for people. For instance, I sometimes need to wash the
feet of a girl in sick bay, and similarly the farm girls enjoy
sluicing my gum-boots on their own initiative - I am taken to the
yard tap regularly when they are in good humour with me. In contrast
nowadays, it is their set task to wait on us extensively, so there
is less scope for spontaneous kindness.

Things grew even worse in August. Looking at late summer and
early autumn as a whole, we lived in increasing chaos, though it was
only during the final few weeks that our ordinary daily routines
reached breaking point. I associate that summer with the noise of
the girls' record-player going full blast, plus the uncontrolled
ringing of the school handbell as it clattered about on the ground,
plus girls keeping their finger on any of numerous bell-pushes for
up to half an hour at a stretch, and worst of all the sound of a
whole roomful of girls in a surge of hysterical, menacing laughter
while Miss Gracey tried to reason them into some sort of order.
They went to see 'Robin Hood', made bows and arrows out of Mr
Marsh's garden lines and bamboo canes, shot them everywhere,
especially at Miss Gracey indoors. Their language was lurid, often
at screaming pitch, even though Miss Gracey offered to write to
Buckingham Palace to let HM know that we were all trying to use the
Queen's English. They threw stones and clods of earth through the
windows from outside, put things in Miss Gracey's food, spat in our
food, kept knives or slivers of broken glass in their bras, and we
had ugly scenes in the garden with sticks, brooms and sickles. They
went through our personal possessions in our bedrooms, and told Miss
Gracey they had drunk champagne in my room (and she may have
believed this for weeks before she learnt direct from me that it
could only have been the dregs of a bottle of Sauternes shared by
the whole staff on a birthday). Later the girls voted for us to
have locks fitted on our bedroom doors, though this still does not
prevent them tooth-combing our private papers, etc., in our locked
bureaux in locked bedrooms.

There was an increase in the atmosphere of hysteria. Some went
constantly but realistically into faints which may have been sham,
sometimes after walking on the roof or guttering, where thankfully
we were not expected to follow them. There was prolonged screaming
and wolf-whistling, they cut and tattoo-ed themselves, even on the
face, refused to eat or to come into meals, sat perched on a farm
gate at night instead of coming to bed, drank disinfectant,
swallowed foreign bodies, obtained doped cigarettes, cut off the
goldfishes' tails and the cats' whiskers, and many other things.

Although much of this was more than ordinary naughtiness, some of it was fathomable but sometimes one felt completely out of one's depth. For example, a new girl, Annette, cut her wrist badly when breaking a window, had it stitched in casualties, and the next day Mr Marsh brought her to me, a bit at a loss, saying the bandage had come off and soil had got into the cut. I took it for granted that Annette would want me to clean and re-bandage her wrist and, apart from my distaste for her wound, I was pleased to be able to tend her constructively, so was nonplussed when she pulled off the new bandage and began picking at the stitches, with a blankly intent face, immediately after I had tried to make her comfortable. It was only with sedation that she let it heal at all. Also, though adolescent screaming is unnerving, it was even more distressing to hear a whole dormitory of girls imitating the crying of babies for long periods at bedtime.

Two incidents were particularly alarming just then. One was Dawn, who, after two days and nights of abnormally violent behaviour, was admitted to the county mental hospital for about three weeks. The most frightening aspect was seeing her carried off by several officials, roped up in a canvas stretcher. She was kept in the hospital's padded cells for five days, but then nurses told us reproachfully that her illness was 'only temper'. During the rest of the three weeks Mrs Briggs and I visited her twice weekly and found the hospital ward comparatively peaceful. The second incident was my happening to discover a small group of girls surrounding and holding Miss Gracey in a remote room upstairs. Most scenes were noisy but this was terrifying in being dead silent. When I entered this private scene, Miss Gracey said calmly: 'Miss Sparrow, will you remove Lynne's hand - she is twisting my key-ring round my finger.' It took me several minutes to prise Lynne off the tortured little finger of Miss Gracey's right hand while other girls held her left arm. She must have been in great pain but did not speak after her initial request. Nobody spoke, either during the incident or about it afterwards. We tend to recount the factual details of incidents but not to mention our fear.

Miss Gracey rarely made a personal remark but told me once that she thought I hated the violence as much as she did herself. I said she kept up appearances pretty well if so, and she replied that she could tell by my eyes. I was doubly surprised because in those clashes there was hardly time even for a habitual eye-searcher (which she was not) to read expressions. My farm clothes are far more suitable for brawling than those of older, indoor staff, and I never went right off my legs - except when I was sent to supervise about ten girls having a snowball fight in the far field and they set on me in a way which we pretended was fun but which left me weak at the knees and stiff for days. In contrast, Miss Gracey was occasionally felled to the floor and it was shocking to catch a glimpse of her rolling there in her good Jaeger suit.

I think the girls themselves were terrified by this time, but unable to stop. All the incidents were 'dealt with' as they cropped up daily, and the atmosphere could change from black to yellow and back again several times a day, but their hatred of Miss Gracey seemed to grow increasingly constant and tangible - a difficult person to imagine being hated. It may have been partly because she

had tried to treat them as sensible grown-ups, and they could not
manage it in the circumstances and turned their resentment back on
her. By late summer she had only to appear or speak in order to
start a scene. They hung in wait for her, chanting 'Nag, nag, nag.'

Looking back, it seems odd that we continued unquestioningly for
so long. My excuses for this are that I did not know what questions
to ask, let alone expect ready answers from outside officials. As a
staff we had no time or energy to discuss what was happening except
to chew over incidents. It took all our time to keep abreast of
events and we had no words for the emotions. To my older
colleagues, the last world war was still close, so our own insular
battles seemed small beer in comparison, and there remained a war-
time spirit of mute endurance plus vague hope of a 'happy issue out
of all our afflictions' - also perhaps some of us had never
visualized ourselves being mixed up in such squalid disruption and
therefore hardly saw that we were. And Miss Gracey's blind faith
was infectious. (On the whole, I am proud to have coped as well as
I did, coming from a sheltered childhood followed by enjoyable bouts
of wildness within harmless limits during student years. It is the
second régime here, as opposed to the first, which taxes the
conscience, with less scope for pride in my work and far more reason
for shame.)

But Miss Gracey's faith seemed obtusely blind, however
idealistic. She did not seem to have her wits about her, being much
more intelligent than the girls but slower on the uptake. She was
often two jumps behind, instead of foreseeing and forestalling
trouble. I felt exasperated, for instance, that she had insufficient nous to learn that using a morning hymn containing the
phrase 'intercourse of hearth and home' would send the girls into a
mass frenzy of giggles on singing the word intercourse. She was
once about to arrange a game she called 'feelers' (identifying
unseen objects in numerous paper bags) until I reminded her that the
word feelers means something different to the girls. Once she was
following Cathy round the house without piecing together Cathy's
repeated route in playing hide and seek, and I inwardly agreed when
Cathy said to me in passing on her defiant escape, 'She's running
round in circles!' She bought a flagpole for the school this
summer, and we had one or two little ceremonies of raising the Union
Jack which ended unpatriotically. Also each department had its own
coloured pennant and these were displayed weekly in order of rank
according to total points awarded for each department's work-
achievement. I longed to hoist a distress signal. (The flagpole
stands stark and unnoticed nowadays.)

Miss Oldham was overworked as Deputy, teacher and being in charge
of clothing. So in the previous spring another teacher was
appointed, Miss Dorcas, a very experienced teacher in other
settings. We had to wait until late October for her to come, and
often said wistfully 'when Miss Dorcas comes...'. In the meantime
Miss Oldham stopped teaching except by remote control. She sat in
the office with Miss Gracey most of the time between scenes - a
friend rather than a wholehearted work-mate. The clothing became
beyond her. Clothes were hidden and lost all over the country,
particularly in neighbouring hedges, the skirts were torn and
custard-encrusted, and the nighties in ribbons (a torn nighty being

a sign of sexual superiority). After the 'changeover', one girl was
found to have fifteen bras, and Gladys had amassed nine staff
pillow-cases on her pillow.

Miss Dorcas came for an introductory weekend towards the end of
the summer. Head and Deputy had forgotten she was coming and were
out with the girls most of the weekend, so I spent most of it
entertaining her - or she entertained me with her extremely
stimulating company. Dorcas, as we came to call her, is a real
character, an excellent teacher, full of outrageously lively ideas,
activities and enthusiasms. She told me later that she found it
hard to forgive me for not warning her then about the state of the
school - she was really interested in moving to 'this work' and came
hoping for great things. I remember being torn about telling her,
and being concerned about the impossibility of a new person starting
under such conditions, but I felt, perhaps wrongly, that it would be
fairer to Miss Gracey to let her find out for herself. I knew she
admired Miss Gracey and agreed in theory with her ideals. Also Miss
Gracey hoped and prayed to the very end that the tide would turn.

Iris Baker and I looked at any applicants for vacant posts with a
view to muscle and weight, because weight is what counts as ballast
in holding violent girls. She and I bought a Judo handbook to make
up for our own deficiencies, but lacked heart to study it. I
learned one hold, 'How to bring in an unwilling prisoner', which
sounded impractical in any case because the first stage requires a
gesture of shaking hands with the prisoner, and proceeding to grip
him in an arm lock. Miss Oldham began to use the half-Nelson in a
rather ruthless way. Tommy is quite weighty, but used to disappear
in the opposite direction of a scene, saying she must go to the loo
first. Mrs Briggs, being elderly, was not allowed to help much but
became expert in clearing plates and implements out of the way. In
one bad brawl in the girls' dining-room, two of us held a farm-girl
who went wild, while others kept the larger group at bay. Many
climbed through the serving-hatch with knives, and Gladys advanced
on Miss Gracey with a huge fish-slice saying, 'I'm going to scalp
her with this.' 'Don't be ridiculous, Gladys,' I said feebly. I
took the farm-girl up to the farm for the rest of our lunch-hour,
hoeing peacefully together, so we escaped the even uglier sequel in
the house where four girls were armed with sharp vegetable knives.
Our school doctor turned up on a routine visit in the midst of it,
and Mrs Briggs told him she was 'seriously concerned for the life of
the headmistress'.

Miss Oldham changed about this time. We relied mainly on her and
had more confidence if she were present. But she became almost
'shell-shocked' - looked ill, and would sit pale and trembling,
unable to help, with occasional bitter crying. She was made to take
extra time off, and it was worse without her. She regained strength
for the very end. Miss Gracey's migraines became more frequent, and
she would fall asleep when she sat down sometimes. I had regular
short holidays at home over 200 miles away, and kept well except for
feeling chronically tired. One morning in early October I felt too
tired to get up and, thinking the farm-girls would manage the pre-
breakfast routine on their own, I sent a message to say I would come
on duty after breakfast. Miss Gracey came and said I was to stay in
bed all day: 'You may not realize it, but you've had a difficult

time, lass!' A few girls popped in and out with bunches of weeds as
presents but otherwise I slept round the clock.

Miss Crandle, whose breezy efficiency remained a by-word, but who
never quite approved of Miss Gracey's methods, left temporarily in
early autumn — saying she felt like a rat deserting a sinking
ship — but returned after the changeover. A caricature of a middle-
aged spinster took her place and left scandalized after a few days.
Miss Alice Sykes, the nicest sort of middle-aged woman, came in her
place — plump and jolly, with a homely northern accent. She came
for interview one awful Wednesday (a day on which I had eight
supervision duties, more than on any other week-day) and I showed
her round. The place was in chaos, screams and swearing kept
floating through the door as I poured tea for her. Miss Sykes had
worked mostly in boys' public schools — this was new to her (not too
new, I hoped) but she said, 'I can see you're in a hole and I'll
start work straightaway.' I grew very fond of her as a good
colleague over the next two years.

We had long since given up regular staff-meetings (the last time
had been when it was discovered that none of the new staff had
signed an Agreement — a fight began before we finished reading our
contracts — we left them lying on the floor and never saw them
again). But we had a short staff-meeting when Miss Sykes came.
Miss Gracey went through the supervision duties, seeming to have
little idea what they entailed, and asked us to undertake them
conscientiously. I was 'on the carpet' only once in Miss Gracey's
reign, for 'leaving the girls' pantry in a disgusting state' after
being on breakfast washing-up duty. It turned out later that a load
of dirty crockery had been sent down from the dormitories after the
main washing-up was complete. By this time, if a girl complained of
feeling unwell, she was allowed to stay in bed — it cut down
numbers. Vanessa used to take dainty trays up to Lynne — wafer-thin
bread and butter, staff china and flowers pinched from Mr Marsh's
green-house. We had few new girls and the numbers dwindled to about
twenty-three.

In the beginning the girls helped us with violence. In the
middle they left us to cope — the best way, I think. Towards the
end they actively opposed us so each incident involved greater
numbers, with half of us trying to keep the bulk at bay. If a girl
did help, she was liable to 'turn' without warning. Four staff
members once struggled lengthily with tall Annette in the entrance
hall and finally began, incredibly slowly and painfully, to carry
her upstairs to detention, two at the head and two at the foot.
Lynne came to help support Annette's middle. About six stairs up,
Lynne suddenly started to scream, 'No you shan't, you shan't', and
we all came down to the bottom much faster than we went up, and had
to begin all over again like Bruce's spider.

Mr Forbes, the only real farmer on the committee, came to discuss
the farm with me one day. As we walked round the fields he said,
'Just tell me confidentially — how are things?' I resented the way
in which they seemed to have washed their hands of us, so replied
coldly: 'If you really want to know, it's bloody hell.' Our former
chairman had resigned and we had a man in her place who lived about
nine miles away. I went for coffee once about now with our former
chairman who had offered me open hospitality at her home, though she

did not mention Downcroft except to say she was 'extremely worried'. Actually they must have been planning underground - for all I know they had special meetings all that summer and autumn to discuss tactics. Meanwhile there was a feeling that we were stranded from the outside world, and we had little contact with any higher authority.

Pearl came as a new girl in early autumn. Apparently she panicked badly on arrival so spent her first day in detention. I met her after tea, when Miss Gracey told me Pearl wanted to join my Young Farmers' Club, meeting the same evening. She took me to be introduced to Pearl in detention, saying we were pretending that Pearl had just arrived, so I shook hands and invited her to come to my Club meeting. Pearl developed an attachment to me which took me quite out of my depth. Her mother had been in a mental hospital since her birth (under the system whereby a dimmish woman having an illegitimate baby can be kept in hospital long-term) and Pearl was supposed never to have had 'a personal relationship'. Gradually there was the suggestion that this relationship with me was her first. I cannot visualize quite how anyone could survive up to the age of fifteen without human relationships, nor could I see how best to start one at that age.

Fortunately perhaps, Pearl seemed to know herself what she wanted. In fact she wanted very little things but in a great quantity every day. She rarely approached me directly, so I may never have exchanged more than a few words with her, but she sent constant messages via other girls. The floor of my corridor was polished more than ever before during her routine early morning housework. If I was off duty before breakfast, I could hear her breathing under the door. Another girl would knock at the door, 'Pearl says good morning, Miss Sparrow.' 'Oh,' I would say from under the bedclothes, 'wish her good morning from me.' Tap, tap a few moments later, and another girl would arrive to say good morning from Pearl. We were very patient in those days. She went through all my personal possessions in my room, either picking the lock or gaining access through the girl who cleaned my room, and left little notes about. By mid-morning, the messages via other girls changed to asking whether I was going to say good-night to Pearl and tuck her up. 'Tell her yes', or occasionally, 'I've already said yes six times today, and she must know by now I always do.' The actual tucking-up took about twenty seconds just before 9.30 p.m. and was only inconvenient in having to return specially when away for the evening off duty. Head and Deputy had an unwritten rule that I was to say good-night to Pearl, otherwise there tended to be an extra outburst. Looking back, it seemed that staff and girls respected this odd little relationship, without actually saying anything, taking it for something more important than an ordinary 'crush'. The only other regular event was that Pearl gave me a bar of chocolate each week after she had gone out to spend her pocket money. Even if slightly burdensome, all this lasted for less than three months - there was a terrible sequel after the changeover.

Alice Sykes settled in fast and got on well with the girls. In late October we stopped saying, 'When Miss Dorcas comes...' because she came. She was not given a very helpful introduction to the schoolroom perhaps. I believe a lot happened there that she never

told us about and she had an intolerable time for the first few
weeks - after that they became really interested in spite of
themselves. On her first morning after prayers, Dorcas went to Miss
Gracey to say she should never have taken prayers with such an
amount of violence and obscenity going on simultaneously. She also
wanted frequent staff-meetings. We had one late at night, and Miss
Gracey kept me back afterwards, wanting to know whether I agreed
with Miss Dorcas's complaint that she (Miss G) was 'too remote from
the staff'. I was surprised and said no (I could have wished her
more remote in a way, though we had fairly little contact with her).

On November the 5th, the farm-girls built a big bonfire with me
and made a Guy. Miss Merton, our inspector, arrived unexpectedly.
Just before dark I went to look at the finished bonfire, to make
sure it was ready for lighting in the evening, and found that the
house-girls had added to it with good shoes, clothes and house-
cleaning equipment. We might not have seen it after dark. In the
evening I drove Miss Merton to the railway station and had a double
gin with her in the station buffet. She said she thought things
were pretty bad, that she was not asking me to tell her anything,
she said she knew. She said she could not do much, 'and it sounds
funny to say this, but the best thing to happen is for Downcroft to
have a riot - then something definite can be done.' Then she hopped
into the train and was borne away. I stood watching it go,
wondering how a riot might be different from existing conditions,
and how soon it might be - half wanting to get it over but dreading
my imaginings of a riot. Iris Baker handed in her notice that day,
saying she would leave straight after Christmas unless someone else
was appointed sooner. Miss Gracey did not appreciate Iris enough.

We had the proper riot on 29 November, although the committee and
inspectors must have decided just beforehand what steps they
intended to take. It was a dreadful week. Miss Gracey drove long
distances most days and had migraines - also she had recently been
bereaved of a relative and had arrangements to make. Taking what I
remember of the seven days of that week: on the first day, Miss
Gracey took Vanessa some distance away to a good job as a kennel
maid. Much spade-work had been done about the job and about her
relationship with Lynne. On the second day, Lynne was spirited away
to another school a long way off - it had been decided at last to
transfer her. That evening, Vanessa telephoned to say she could not
or would not stay in her new job - I think she had already arranged
with Lynne to come back within days. Miss Gracey brought her back,
and had a bad journey after she had broken the news that Lynne had
gone - they talked in the car for a long time on arrival back here.

On the third or fourth day, about 9 p.m., Annette was found
trying to strangle her 'best mate', Marion, who was hurt and
terrified. Annette had a kind of hysterical fit immediately
afterwards, and we carried her to an empty staff bedroom to lie on
the bed. She screamed abuse at Miss Gracey for what seemed like
about 1½ hours, before the doctor sedated her. I went to see how
Marion was, in her dormitory - it was quite mad. Marion lay mutely
wide-eyed, there was a couple petting, others quarrelling, one had
thrown a trayful of crockery out of the window, and another was
reading the Bible aloud with a sanctimonious expression to a deaf
audience. Meanwhile, when Annette quietened, Miss Gracey took her

somewhere else to talk to her. It was very late by this time. We
did not know where they were, so waited in the staff-room or perhaps
had supper. Suddenly we heard Annette screaming on the landing,
hysterical again, 'I've done her in, I've done her in at last...'.
We looked hastily all over the house for Miss Gracey, and I found
her in Miss Oldham's bedroom. She was lying on the hearthrug and I
thought she was dead for a moment. We revived her quite quickly
from what she said was a black-out – it may well have been, and
Annette could have been shocked into believing she herself had
caused it.

On the fifth day, Lynne was seen in the bushes, having absconded
from her new school. Vanessa ran out to her on hearing the news,
and they absconded together. I did not expect them to return, as
Lynne no longer belonged to us. On the morning of the sixth day,
that is the day of the so-called riot, things were fairly quiet
apart from a struggle with Annette, but there was an atmosphere.
After 'prayers' Miss Gracey kept the girls back to talk to them. I
went over to the farm to start work – it was becoming increasingly
difficult to get through the essential farm routine. At about
9.30-9.45 the farm-girls set off for the farm but did not arrive. I
was cleaning out the pigs, and did not know it was different from
any other morning. The people in the house knew by this time that
Vanessa and Lynne were hiding in our coal-house, having returned
about breakfast-time. Girls had thrown blankets to them from the
windows, and given them food, staff clothes and money. The police
were summoned to collect Lynne. When they arrived, the two girls
escaped, plus more than half the school.

I knew nothing of this, until I went to look for my girls, and
saw a police-woman impaled on a strand of barbed wire. Then I heard
a tremendous noise at the far end of the fields and went up. This
was the first half of the riot. There were numerous policemen, and
struggling girls, and the air blue with swearing. The boundary
fence and hedge were broken down, with girls on both sides. We (the
remaining staff) like to recount 'what we did in the riot'. I did
little, and Mr Marsh thinks he coped with the only girl I think I
dealt with. He extracted her from the mob and, as she was the most
difficult of my current farm-girls, I took her to the farm, and
settled her down to work, before returning to the house.
Simultaneously the police caught Vanessa and Lynne, and returned to
the house surrounded by an angry mob. Perhaps the first half
happened earlier – I don't know.

As I reached the house, Miss Oldham met me and said it was over,
and asked me to be ready to receive girls in my own department.
There had been a big scene in the house – Rosie on a policeman's
back, Miss Gracey being told she had never had a 'lover' and did not
understand, and a good deal of crockery was smashed. Nobody was
much hurt; one police-woman had a dislocated thumb. It is amazing
how little people are hurt, considering. The sergeant rang central
government to report a riot, but Miss Gracey took the receiver out
of his hand, saying it was now under control. The police took Lynne
away and we did not see her again. It was also amazing to me that
we had normal school dinner at the end of the morning, having
completed our routine farm work in a strange atmosphere. Secretly I
was relieved that the riot seemed to have happened, and that it was
nothing out of this world.

Two inspectors arrived after lunch to attend the usual monthly
committee meeting - this must have been planned beforehand. All was
quiet on the farm. Apparently Mr Marsh and I were criticized for
losing our girls in the riot, but as they had never arrived and we
knew nothing, I did not feel blameworthy. I felt more angry that
one of the inspectors was said to have been 'poorly' afterwards
through his distress over the riot at which he was not present.
After the meeting, I drove the committee chairman to his home with
polite general conversation on the way. I returned to Downcroft to
find Miss Oldham nearly fainting and in tears. Miss Gracey had been
told after the meeting, from which she was excluded, that she was
dismissed, and due to leave a week hence on 5 December. Most of the
girls were to be transferred. A senior worker from a similar school
elsewhere was to come on 5 December to take over as Acting Head.
Miss Oldham immediately gave in her own notice although she was
asked to reconsider it.
    Miss Gracey took the news with her usual courage, but still
wanted further discussion with the committee. They refused. She
asked for my opinion the following morning - the seventh day of that
week - perhaps she hoped the staff would appeal on her behalf. I
was unable to say much - I was desperately sorry about her
personally (she could not have coped with sympathy) but relieved
otherwise. In the afternoon, she and Miss Oldham took all the girls
for a long walk. Dorcas and I went for a walk by ourselves to a
village about three miles away - a long, straight road on a grey
day. We talked, and in a ridiculous way it was like the walk to
Emmaus - or alternatively, like a death in the family after a long,
painful illness, because most of the staff were numb, shattered but
also perhaps secretly relieved as I was.
    Miss Gracey told the girls at some point she was leaving. They
took it quite nicely but were difficult during the week. We were
unable to assemble the girls together for about the last fortnight.
We had another minor 'riot' during the final week, which I cannot
bother to describe now. It took place in the grounds from after
breakfast until nearly mid-morning and I was there by myself much of
the time, extracting individual girls from the hubbub. It seemed to
start for the trivial reason that Miss Dorcas had preceded me out of
the girls' dining-room after breakfast, and the girls saw me as
senior though I was junior in all but the length of time served
here. Anyway, Miss Sykes popped her head out of the kitchen door
during the scrum and said, 'Eh, Birdy, find Dorcas - they've
kidnapped her.' Dorcas turned up soon after, not wanting to say
what had happened.
    During the final part of that morning, we attempted the routine
work normally completed earlier. So when Freda, usually docile,
refused to clean the cowshed, I told them it was becoming impossible
to run a farm under these conditions, and that Freda was going to
clean the cowshed if it was the last thing she or I did. I stood
over her after the other girls had gone to dinner and she eventually
said I was getting on her nerves and took up a pitchfork as a
weapon. I closed in, on the same principle as it being safer to
keep close rather than at leg's length of a kicking cow, but was
shocked in a few moments to find my hands were round her throat.
Mr Marsh and Bill happened to hear us from nearby; Freda calmed down

when she saw she was outnumbered and we cleaned the cowshed together
in fairly amicable silence.

The rest of the week was very uncomfortable. Miss Gracey got her
office work up-to-date over several nights, and packed. The
chairman and ex-chairman came one evening to see all the staff,
asking us to give our loyal support to the new Acting Head, Mrs
Strang. They may have gathered from Miss Oldham that we intended to
be awkward over Miss Gracey's dismissal. On 5 December a removal
van took away Miss Gracey's furniture and luggage. The girls stood
about clapping and cheering. Iris tried to get her rooms cleaned
quickly ready for Mrs Strang. I persuaded a farm-girl to clean Miss
Gracey's car, and find a box to put her kitten in. It was an awful
day. Miss Gracey did not leave until 5 p.m. and Mrs Strang was due
at 5.40. She went into tea to say good-bye to the girls, who showed
regret over losing one of several kittens. She left us each a small
bunch of flowers, put her head quickly round the staff room door,
said 'Goodbye, folk', and drove quickly away.

For a few moments we sat in silence and then realized the school
was in a bit of an uproar. Miss Oldham dried her eyes and put all
the girls on to housework, and they settled. Most of the staff
thought it would take the Angel Gabriel to straighten things out and
that, even if it were possible, we had a hard struggle ahead. Mrs
Briggs and I had walked round the house a day or two previously,
visualizing it with a newcomer's eyes, and saw that it was dirty and
much knocked about. At 5.30 p.m. I brushed my hair, powdered my
nose and sat down to wait for Mrs Strang. I had looked forward to
her coming but suddenly felt too tired and overwhelmed to start the
next phase.

CHAPTER 5

Mrs Strang arrived punctually to the dot, with a flotilla of two
committee members who showed her round the house, where girls were
working with eyes on stalks, then introduced her to the staff, and
left us to carry on. She breezed in to us with a mixture of
forceful diffidence, a broad smile on her plain, strong face. She
seemed enormous. Having told us her plan for the evening, she went
to unpack. We sat, on our best behaviour. Miss Oldham said
dispiritedly, 'Well, she radiates strength anyway.' Bill Evans
caught a glimpse of her arrival, and ran excitedly to tell Mr Marsh
that the Queen of Tonga had come.

She came down for supper (dinner for staff, when the girls always
have a lighter snack following high tea) in severely impeccable
clothes. When the supper bell rang, she punched one fist into her
palm, said 'Right - now for it!' and strode off to meet the girls.
She and Miss Oldham took supper with the girls, while we strained
our ears in the staff dining-room. The girls seemed unnaturally
quiet, but apparently the meal did not run quite smoothly, because
Miss Oldham was soon asked to leave the room, while Mrs Strang
addressed the school. She gave them several short, blunt speeches
during the next few days. We did not know the gist, except for one
remark: 'Miss Gracey was too good for you - now you've got ME, and
you're going to feel the difference.'

At 9.30 p.m. we had a short staff-meeting, mostly about practical
matters and the remnants of our daily routine. She thanked those of
us who were off duty for attending, and in general treated us as
people of importance, worthy of consideration. As someone said
later, 'We are the STAFF!' The only jarring note was her mentioning
casually the use of 'the theatrical slap, with a stiff hand, which
sounds loud but doesn't hurt'. As none of us had ever slapped a
girl's face, this seemed unthinkable and I did not visualize it
actually happening. I was more impressed by the exceptionally
gentle way in which Mrs Strang picked up our tabby kitten at the end
of the meeting.

I shall never forget next morning at prayers. The girls stood
rigidly in precise rows with perfect behaviour. We stood in a row
at the back. The volume of Mrs Strang's singing voice was
startling, and we all sang as if our lives depended on it. The

strangeness and contrast kept coming over me in waves and I
struggled against weak giggles. It transpired that one girl had
sniggered (silently from nervousness, I imagined). Mrs Strang had
never known such a thing: 'In future, any girl sniggering in prayers
will have another two months put on her time before she is even
considered for discharge.' The farm- and garden-girls were
dismissed for morning work. They made 'too much noise' so were
called back and sent again. They lined up in twos silently at the
back door and marched over to the farm in an exaggerated way. I ran
behind, quite dazed, not sure whether Mrs Strang would approve or
not. Things were much the same on the farm, except that we no
longer seemed to know each other quite so well.

During the morning I was summoned urgently to the office.
Apparently there was not to be a large transfer of girls (the market
being already somewhat saturated by our cast-offs) but Mrs Strang
felt she could not 'clear up the school' with Annette in it. She
arranged Annette's removal forthwith. Plans, down to the last
detail, had been made that very morning. I was to drive, with Miss
Oldham and Bill as escorts, setting off at 1.15 p.m. Mrs Briggs and
Dorcas were to take the whole school for a long walk at 1.00 p.m. so
that they should not observe the departure, and Annette was to
travel in her nightdress under sedation. The strangest thing to me
was that Mrs Strang showed more nervousness over one doped girl than
did Miss Gracey when far outnumbered. The three of us delivered
Annette safely some hours later - a pathetic, straggly waif for all
her physical height, seeming more disturbed than when she first came
to us. We then found ourselves free in London. We half felt we
should hurry back in case of need, but Miss Oldham insisted on an
immediate leisurely dinner. This seemed to be the first meal we had
enjoyed peacefully for weeks, and I ordered a double helping of the
main course. On return, the day's events sounded very mild.

The following day Mrs Strang came to see round the farm. She
told me she was very pleased indeed by it and that I could tell my
girls so. During that week I think one girl was slightly awkward,
so Mrs Strang assembled everybody and spoke forcibly on required
standards of behaviour. Consciously I was absolutely 'with' her,
and could have sworn that I kept a poker face, but she sent for me
afterwards to enquire why I disapproved. I felt unable to explain
that I disliked the cheap and common way in which she spoke to the
girls. I took it for granted that she had integrity and liked
someone who called a spade a spade. I think the whole school felt
secure in the presence of a person who was short and sharp, who
meant what she said in few words, and with whom 'you knew where you
were'. We greatly appreciated the novelty of being looked straight
in the eye, having the butter passed at meal-times, and having a
warm personal interest taken in us.

I think Mrs Strang came anxious to get on well with the staff.
We felt rather apologetic about being part of the team that had
'failed' - she bolstered our morale and somehow reinstated us as The
Staff in the eyes of the girls. This was delicate - I suppose it
was necessary but one felt further away from them. I do wish I had
thought more of the girls' feelings in all this. I imagine that
with being tired myself and bewildered by the sudden changeover, and
having lived in extreme fear for months, I did not realize that they

must be feeling exactly the same. They had been terrified into
rebelling (though it looked like deliberate defiance at the time)
and were now terrified into submission, though there was the feeling
that they might break out again at any moment. The sudden
silence - one hardly knew there were girls in the house - was almost
as unnerving as the previous noise. We had got ourselves into an
incredible mess but now Mrs Strang salvaged us with an ease and
swiftness exceeding our highest hopes, so we really had to trust
her. I certainly did.
    Evidently Miss Merton stressed to Mrs Strang the importance of
'mothering the staff' (perhaps foreseeing difficulties) which she
undertook with her usual thoroughness and which was comforting. Her
initial attitude to me was 'the child's worn out', although she
seemed to rely on us a good deal. I felt there was a chance now to
do some really positive work on the farm. Mrs Strang has high
standards and seemed initially to be an excellent organizer. She
told us her likes and dislikes: she likes 'straight dealing' and
dislikes 'spaniels', smut and swearing (hell, damn and blast being
the only expletives she allows herself. The girls' swearing soon
diminished after one or two mouths were washed out.) I became more
businesslike and began to copy her habit of doing things immediately
if not sooner. Most of the staff and girls fell over themselves in
their haste to obey an order. It had not been apparent that Miss
Gracey had bells in her office, bedroom and sitting-room (except
that she used to lean on the office one accidentally) but now they
rang constantly and Mrs Strang kept her finger on the bell-push for
several seconds. She also strode about the house, even after
lights-out, with a firm, measured tread - in contrast to our
previous discreet tip-toes. The only raised voice one heard was her
own.
    Mrs Strang decided to take all meals with the girls by herself
for the first few weeks. This alone was enough to endear her to us.
So we found ourselves an unusually big party in the staff dining-
room. Mrs Strang was determined to nourish us - we had enormous
breakfasts of porridge, bacon and eggs. She herself suffers from
duodenal ulcers and has to watch her diet. For the first time some
of the staff slightly irritated me at mealtimes. The gusty
breathing of Alice Sykes, and the shrill squeaks of Dorcas's crêpe-
soled shoes swivelling enthusiastically on the polished floor,
annoyed me. Although Alice had known Miss Gracey only a short time,
she could not get over the cruelty of her dismissal. We went over
and over the same arguments every mealtime. I minded very much for
Miss Gracey, but thought it inevitable and too late for further
agonizing now. At the same time I felt vaguely guilty in being so
easily 'off with the old and on with the new'.
    On the other hand, we were reproached mildly about our
irresponsibility and misplaced loyalty in having protected Miss
Gracey for so long. This was a new and upsetting idea to me: that
one was able to report information about senior colleagues to higher
authorities. Mrs Strang was emphatic in making clear that we were
in future to go straight to the committee with any dissatisfactions
about her leadership. Eventually I conceded, but said we would tell
her first, and laughed openly at the unlikelihood of such a
contingency! After a few days Dorcas went to have coffee with a

committee member. Before she went I said, 'Tell Mrs Percy everything in the garden's lovely.' 'Oh,' said Dorcas, 'you do approve,
do you. I thought I was the only one who is 100 per cent.' 'Of
course I do,' I replied, 'only I don't make a song about it'
(thinking of her crêpe-soled shoes). Apparently Dorcas had told Mrs
Strang she was prepared to work shoulder-to-shoulder with her,
without time off, until Downcroft was 'cleared up'. Mrs Strang
welcomed this good offer, called her 'brother' and kept her on the
hop. Her hopping was a little wearing; also she and Iris Baker
irritated each other excessively about keys.

Another surprising thing was that the aspects I had expected us
to tackle seemed to disappear automatically, but a great deal of
time was spent in sorting material things, such as the clothing, and
a mound of tangled knitting wool as big as a haycock. Dorcas was
visualized as future Deputy after the departure of Miss Oldham, who
was quietly humble and seemed past caring – she was released early
from her notice 'on medical grounds'. It was sad to see her go, a
shadow of her former self, a person whose contribution might have
been even more valuable had she legitimately held, rather than
withheld, the reins. Mrs Briggs continued in the same cart-rut of
common sense, 'keeping her own countenance'. I was frequently out
in the van, chauffering and running errands, so saw less of the
staff, but we all seemed a bit edgy, probably because the worst was
over.

On my way upstairs to my first dormitory-duty under the new
régime, I met Mrs Strang. 'I hope you don't tuck the girls in,' she
said in a peculiarly menacing way, 'if you do, I'll tuck you in.'
Startled, I said no. But after dormitory-duty – when none of the
girls, not even Pearl, asked to be tucked in, apparently having been
told it was now forbidden – I went back to Mrs Strang to say that in
fact I was in the habit of tucking them up, and could see no harm in
it. (We had all been in the habit, on request.) She explained
quite kindly that I, in my innocence, might see no harm, but there
is, and the practice must cease. We could not, she said, be too
careful 'after all the trouble of that sort' there had been in the
school. Though unable to see any homosexual aura in tucking
bedclothes maternally, I felt equally unable to make a special plea
for Pearl. The very fact that it was special made it awkward to
plead. There were suddenly strict rules about girls touching each
other at all or going anywhere near each others' beds. Mrs Strang
went on to say that we must all be very careful too not to arouse
any suspicions amongst the girls about staff relationships. She
intended to retire to her rooms early at night, and strongly advised
us not to entertain colleagues in our rooms either – would I inform
the staff. Hitherto we had done little or no 'entertaining',
largely through lack of sociable opportunities. Alice Sykes did not
understand this new veto-cum-advice – I tried to explain delicately,
and the penny eventually dropped with a disgusted clang.

On one of the first Sundays it was planned that I should drive
alone to Mallingham to see whether Gladys's aunt would give her a
permanent home. Mrs Strang had not been able to make much
impression on Gladys. Late the previous evening Miss Oldham flared
briefly with her former spirit, and told Mrs Strang it was wrong to
expect me to drive over 300 miles in my present weariness. Mrs

Strang sent for me, quite cross, saying she could tell by my face
that I wanted to go, but that I would not be asked to drive again if
I returned tired. She saw herself as my champion and it was
uncomfortable to have Head and Deputy bickering over my welfare.
Foolishly, I took the warning seriously, and flew to Mallingham and
back like one possessed, in my anxiety to return early and fresh. I
reeled on emerging from the unwieldy van, but fortunately this went
unobserved, and the news that her aunt was willing to have Gladys
was greeted with general delight. About a week later I took Gladys
by train, on my way further north for a brief holiday. Our luggage
included numerous cartons and carrier-bags representing the odd
hoardings of Gladys's life sans staff pillow-cases - a porter took
one look at us and muttered, 'Where my caravan hath rested'.

   Before I went Iris Baker told me that she would go mad if Dorcas
did not stop interfering with her work in the house - the only time
I saw Iris incensed. I asked Dorcas to give her some peace. She
agreed, and said she would write if anything important happened
while I was away. (We still half-feared a massive worm-turning of
girls.) Quite soon, I received a surprising letter from Dorcas, who
had been over 100 per cent, if anything, when I left. Apparently,
after working for a fortnight non-stop, she had mentioned time off.
Immediately she was 'blasted up' to her room and 'a supper-tray was
blasted up' after her. She said the girls had worked wonders for
Mrs Strang in a fortnight but that she continued to blast. If this
went on (a) the girls or (b) the staff or (c) Mrs S would crack....
Mrs Strang interviewed me in the office on my return. There was now
no question of Dorcas becoming Deputy - the post would be
advertised - but in the meantime Dorcas and I were to be Joint
Acting Deputies. Nobody would remember this now - I hardly do
myself - not that I did much during temporary promotion except be
somewhat officious. From then on, Dorcas (always bursting with
nervous energy) was not allowed to put in a moment's extra time over
her formal duty hours - very galling for her.

   We had an extremely quiet, well ordered but fairly happy
Christmas 19X5. On New Year's Eve, Mrs Briggs and I drove to
Blymouth to collect an 'old girl' from the police-station there. We
rushed back for midnight but found there were no celebrations. Miss
Crandle had returned to take charge of housework. I was very sorry
when Iris left but have managed to keep in touch.

   The girls had been very quiet indeed for a month. This
unbelievably good behaviour, as I saw it, lasted pretty well into
the following summer of 19X6. They were seen but not heard.
Indoors they went about in orderly single file. The farm-girls even
said 'excuse me' to the cows. The staff were taking turns to be on
duty alone in the girls' dining-room. Vanessa was Head Girl!

CHAPTER 6

Harmony calved early in January. The outcome seemed uncertain as it
was her first venture after her accident. She started on a Saturday
morning. I told Mrs Strang I would be late for lunch and asked
permission to keep my farm-girls. Some of our cows like an audience
when they calve, others prefer not, but in daylight they have to
tolerate slight loss of privacy because the girls so much enjoy
being present. On this occasion Mrs Strang organized me, with
unnecessarily complex good will. My lunch arrived incongruously
elegant on a tray. I did not want inexperienced, non-farm girls
around, in case delivery was difficult or the calf dead, but Mrs
Strang sent a crowd of extra 'helpers' and changed into slacks
herself. In the event Harmony managed easily, producing a healthy
heifer calf whom we call Highlight, at 2.30 p.m. Mrs Strang arrived
just in time to see the final stages, but afterwards believed
Harmony leaned heavily on her throughout.

Bill Evans was interested, so before my tea-time duty I went to
his cottage to give him the news and we decided to celebrate quickly
in the evening. His wife pressed two glasses of home-made wine on
me before tea, and I must say my tea-duty alone with the girls was
the least nerve-racking meal enjoyed with them for a long time. I
visualized one drink at the pub later, and bought the first round of
half-bitters. Bill treated us to a second round and a friend of his
to a third. Normally I could have taken this, but with being sleepy
and then emerging into a frosty night for the walk home, I felt
distinctly odd, and had to concentrate extremely hard during staff
supper. Colleagues assured me afterwards that I'd behaved
perfectly, if a little argumentatively with Mrs Strang, when the
latter sent for me. Several girls were going on leave next day and
she kept me running about with preparations. When I made a foolish
remark, which I might have made anyway, about the train time-table,
she said 'What is the matter with you, child?' I said lightly I'd
had slightly too much beer, not dreaming she would think I am ever
actually drunk, but she referred to students of my former University
as having 'a bad reputation for drinking'. I have learnt since how
alarmingly easy it is to acquire a doubtful reputation in the
educational establishment of Downcroft.

Anyway, it is certain that I enjoyed the highest reputation at

this stage. Mrs Strang saw me through rose-coloured spectacles
during her first few months. I was quite wonderful in nearly every
direction and could do anything - an excellent farmer, very good
with the girls (just a shade soft), a competent driver, good at
looking after the staff, and had good manners. I was not entirely
taken in but rather thrived on my reputation. She even used me to
perform various feats of physical strength in the house, such as
opening intractable ink-bottles, although I am really quite puny,
and yet I seemed always to succeed somehow (by knack if not by
brawn), almost by virtue of my reputation which seemed to work like
Samson's hair. After the early months she alternated between rose
and shaded glasses, mostly rose first and then mostly shaded.
During the last two years it has been through dark glasses. On
reading this, it seems fair to add that I have employed a parallel
range of spectacles in regarding her, and it is a pity our mutual
eyesight is so coloured.

The interviews for appointing a new headmistress were in late
January. Mrs Strang was extremely (almost embarrassingly) anxious
to be offered the post. We were equally anxious that she should.
We had confidence in her; we felt she deserved it after doing the
dirty work of 'clearing up the school', and we felt sure that if
someone less able were chosen things would be as bad as before after
this brief lull. We did not feel able to face that again. The day
before the appointment, I had to see our committee treasurer in
Glebe about farm business. Towards the end he said he wanted to ask
me in confidence whether I thought Mrs Strang was ill-treating the
girls. I said no, she was very strict but had needed to be so, and
I imagined she would relax once proper order was restored. He said
it was important for the committee to be sure, and that somebody,
Mrs Pemberton in fact, had complained on these lines. Mrs Pemberton
is a local part-time worker who comes to help with games and
clerical aspects. I was vaguely annoyed that she, not living or
teaching at Downcroft, could pronounce judgment on Mrs Strang while
being so affable to her face.

I would give a lot not to have done this next thing. I'm ashamed
of having broken a confidence and also it has caused me much
backwash. Anyway, after rapid thought, I told Mrs Strang what the
treasurer had said. My reasons for telling her were: (a) I knew she
was worked-up and thought she might lose her nerve if suddenly
charged with ill-treatment at her interview next day; (b) I hoped
she would ease up a bit as soon as possible; (c) it would not stop
her being asked but I thought it fair to warn her; (d) she was being
all honey to me and people seem unable to see her unkindness to
others when she is nice to them personally; (e) self-importance. As
soon as she had extracted the essential information from me she
rushed off. An hour or so later, she asked whether I had any idea
who had made the allegation. I thought I gave the impression that I
knew but wouldn't say; her impression was that I didn't know. I
took it for granted that she would respect the fact that I'd been
asked in confidence - of course she didn't. Not that I was in a
position to ask her to, having broken it myself. She must then have
rushed off to confide in Mrs Pemberton! The latter in turn tackled
me privately: 'You are a fool, Birdy - I told the committee that.'
'Yes,' I said, 'and I wish you hadn't. But you needn't worry that I

shall tell her you did.' Mrs Pemberton told the treasurer what I'd
done (he thought I was afraid of Mrs Strang) and the wretched thing
went round in a vicious circle. Years later, Mrs S realized
(through my silence under further questioning) that I'd known the
identity of the person making the allegation from the beginning, and
by that time she felt I had double-crossed her from the start by
withholding information.

Next day I met the other candidates while showing them round the
farm. None inspired confidence. One outraged me - a youngish woman
with no experience of anything to do with 'the work', who laughingly
confessed that she'd applied 'just for the hell of it'. 'Yes, hell
for everybody', I felt like replying. Mrs Strang was full of
butterflies and temperament, but in the end was offered the job.
She'd thought it touch and go because the ill-treatment question had
indeed arisen. I think Mrs Pemberton shook hands with her when she
told us her triumphant news. Later that evening Mrs Strang said
shyly to me, 'I'm not one to gush, but I would like to thank
you...'. I am sure she would have been appointed even if I had been
in Timbuctoo, and I quite wish now I had been many miles away.

Life continued much as before, perhaps a little less questionably
now that the position was confirmed. Mrs Strang immediately took 1½
days off, having had no change hitherto, and stressing her need to
get away from all of us. On her return, which we heard, we could
easily have invited her into the staff sitting-room where we were
having tea, but we refrained, remembering her wish for complete
seclusion. Her reaction was to say that as nobody had heard her
return, anybody could enter unnoticed, so in future the front door
must be locked at 4 p.m. (very inconvenient but difficult to argue).
She constantly makes snap rules of this sort. If something happens
once, she reacts as though it must be guarded against for evermore.

The new prefect system was difficult to adjust to. Previously
the school assembled in order of seniority, with newest girls at the
front. The girl most senior in time had been Head Girl, other
seniors had more responsibility but there were no prefects as such.
Now we had proper prefects, chosen by Mrs Strang from any level, and
a Head Girl with considerable power. As Vanessa still had a good
deal of surreptitious influence, it was as well for her to hold an
official position I suppose. The prefects seem highly important.
It is difficult to uphold their position and one's own simultaneously. Without care, they are liable to take charge. They work
directly under the headmistress so, even with great care, they are
under orders to report every incident to her, whether or not it has
been dealt with by the member of staff concerned.

Kim is an example of how the girls changed in appearance. She
had been quite glamorous, with long hair bleached at the ends, and
wore her uniform with a jaunty air. She was transformed in a few
weeks - mousey hair cut short, straight and unshaped, and National
Health spectacles. She dressed soberly and wore her beret at a
ridiculously old-fashioned angle, according to regulations. She
also developed a servile manner. In Miss Gracey's time Tommy cut
individuals' hair attractively on request. Nowadays a hairdresser
does regulation crops en masse on her monthly visit. They pay for
it out of their pocket money with secret resentment. Mrs Strang's
reasoning is that it prevents their claiming a member of staff has

cut off their hair as a punishment. Similarly, they are no longer allowed to buy small presents for staff, in case they say they have been forced to spend money on us. 'Ann brought this back for you, Miss Sparrow,' said Mrs S, when the first set of girls returned from home-leave. 'Oh,' I said, not sure whether to thank Ann or not, as her little present of a cigarette-holder clattered into the waste-paper basket.

Mrs Strang worries terribly about people's comments on her. Miss Gracey was blissfully unaware of danger in girls or staff 'talking', and saw no reason for fear in her dealings with girls' parents, committee, inspectors, newspaper reporters or MPs. I used to say glibly to Mrs Strang, 'If it's not true, why worry?' My former 'innocence' included ignorance of there being any significance in having things 'in black and white' (i.e. on paper) or in 'having a witness' to ordinary conversation. We soon realized that a continued relationship with Miss Gracey was considered undesirable from Mrs Strang's viewpoint. But Miss Gracey yearned for news of Downcroft in a completely unsubversive way. I wrote twice to her, and was tackled about my correspondence. I remember saying politely and calmly to Mrs S, 'Perhaps there are grounds in this case, but normally I'd say you had no need to enquire into our relationships outside the school.' In her early days, I got away with saying many risky things, simply because I was unaware of being on wafer-thin ice - by the time I knew, she was far more likely to take umbrage even with delicate hints, just because she knew I knew.

By February the staff began to relax after lights-out. Mrs Strang was closeted asexually upstairs and the girls were asleep. We had not let ourselves go for a long time. Miss Crandle, Dorcas and Alice Sykes could be very funny - we often laughed till the tears rolled down our cheeks. Later we were asked to tone down our laughter but it was very pleasant while it lasted. We were bound to speculate a little about Mr Strang, of whom nothing is known, except that it seemed to have been a brief union, without issue. We slowly developed the hypothesis that Mr Strang had been eaten, apart from his toothbrush moustache, during his initial attempt to consummate the marriage. These and other themes clearly provoked ribald laughter. I enjoy 'vulgarity' when it is spontaneously funny. In contrast, Mrs Strang's serious preoccupation with sordid smutless sex is quite offputting.

Dorcas asserted that it is the spice of life to discuss other people, and said she made it all right by first saying to the person's face what she intended to say behind their back. I half-admired her candour, but could not imagine how she managed to tell Alice Sykes that she had a hole in her head, or Miss Crandle that she was like a dog which returned to its vomit (having resigned, then returned to work here), or Tommy that she was more of a liability than the girls, not to mention Mrs Strang thinking she is God. But one day, in the midst of a friendly conversation, talking nineteen to the dozen, Dorcas said to me, 'Though of course you mightn't agree, being amoral and completely unprincipled', and rattled on - ignoring my protest, 'Stop a minute, Dorcas, what was that you said?' with a Mona Lisa smile while she continued to buzz hypnotically. At least I now knew how she achieved such frankness! By this time Dorcas sadly was disillusioned in her great desire to

work constructively here. (Although she stayed for less than five
months in all, she certainly made her mark, and indeed is instru-
mental in my leaving now, 3½ years later.) Mrs Strang sympathized
with me once or twice early on about Dorcas's 'unpleasant attitude'
to me, arising through jealousy she thought. I disagreed, feeling
on fairly easy terms with Dorcas, and explaining that the only
possible reason for any unease, as I saw it, was that Dorcas might
well think anyone who fitted into both contrasting régimes as
comfortably as I did must be insincere, and that I did wonder
myself. I pondered this aloud so earnestly that I was unaware of
its tactless implication to Mrs Strang, though she was unable to see
the point in any case.
    During the early weeks Pearl's mutely eager face was a constant
reproach to me. In fact what happened with her was my first cause
for real inward discomfort under the new régime. Her incessant
messages via other girls ceased abruptly after the changeover.
Instead, she occasionally approached me directly, only for a split
second, appearing and disappearing breathlessly round a corner, each
time whispering urgently the same message: 'I'm being good, Miss
Sparrow, I'm being good.' She gave me little chance to reply,
unless to say, 'Take it gently, then, Pearl', or even flippantly,
'Don't strain yourself then'. It is only too tempting to be
flippant in the face of such painfully deaf and dumb struggles to
communicate. She still left an occasional little note in my
bedroom, and I became vaguely uneasy through their increasingly
passionate quality - for instance 'Yours always if you like',
scrawled on my newspaper, made me wonder what Mrs Strang would
think, though my own feeling now is that there was nothing very
'queer' in Pearl's longing to belong to someone.
    Two or three photographs were missing from my locked desk, photos
either of me or me with my ex-fiancé, and it was rumoured among the
girls that Pearl had at least one of them in her possession. I
think a prefect reported this to Mrs Strang - certainly I would
prefer to think it was no casual comment of mine which led to Mrs
Strang's interrogation of Pearl. The first I knew of it was one
evening when I was alone in the staff sitting-room and Mrs Strang
entered briefly, without a word, to remove the coal-tongs. A few
moments later Mrs Strang returned in ominously grim triumph, holding
at arm's length in the tongs a limp rag, which she threw on the
fire. 'That's all that's left of your photograph! Don't ask me
what she's been doing with it. You won't want it back - fire's the
best place for it.' 'What has she been doing with it?'
'Masturbating with it.' Thoroughly shaken, I began to digest this
in silence. 'Is she very upset?' 'Not she. Don't expect her to
have any decent feeling such as you might have. She's only upset at
being found out. When you've been in the work half as long as I
have, Sparrow, you'll know that you simply cannot afford to be soft.
Give them an inch and they'll take a mile. Anyway, I've told her in
no uncertain terms she's to have nothing more to do with you.
That's the end. I will see to Miss Pearl from now on.' No more was
said, at least not to me. Having always felt slightly out of my
depth with Pearl's intense but indirect attachment, I was quite
unable now to explain, let alone fight for, her apparent need of me.
She seemed to retreat into limbo with a correctly blank face. In

the following weeks, I tried to behave naturally to her as one of
the group, but it was unmistakable that whatever feeling she once
cherished had been killed stone dead.   She knew it was all up,
whatever efforts I might have made.   To do her justice, Mrs Strang
did seem, in her fashion, to take some pains in cultivating Pearl,
who may or may not have gained comfort during the short time this
attention lasted.

   It is necessary to stress that we still felt, and long continued
to feel, considerable relief under the new reign.   Also, as in my
early weeks under Miss Gracey's leadership, the incidents so far
described (by no means all) were widely interspersed with
comparative calm.   What is puzzling is that, although fear abounded
in both régimes, the plain physical fear of the first was far easier
to meet than the mixture of blatant and subtle conflicts of the
second.   I would not be puzzled at all except for having discovered
through direct experience here that I am more a physical than a
moral coward, though unfortunately it is only too clear that I have
insufficient strength to stand by my own beliefs consistently.

CHAPTER 7

Early in March Mrs Strang was away for nearly three days at a
Conference on 'The Work' (which is our exclusive term for our
particular job of 'bringing on backward souls'). The staff were
quite nervous to be left holding the fort, but the girls were most
co-operative, and our individual responsibilities were minutely
detailed on a large typed notice so we had little scope for straying
off the straight and narrow. Mrs Briggs seemed honoured to be
entrusted with organizing the 'mid-week knicker change'. Just
before I drove her to the station, Mrs Strang handed me what she
called a Staff Meeting Book, saying she had not been able to fit in
a proper staff-meeting so would I read these notes to the staff that
evening. I agreed and put the book aside without looking at it. On
the way to the station, she asked me out of the blue whether I find
it difficult to make decisions. I answered vaguely, never having
thought about it, and not finding inspiration to say it surely
depends on how difficult the decisions themselves are.
     At 9.30 p.m. I started reading 2½ pages of notes in the Book to
my friends Mrs Briggs, Miss Crandle, Tommy, Dorcas and Alice,
growing increasingly uncomfortable as I did so. It consisted of a
long list of things the staff were asked to do or not to do, written
in a somewhat terse style. I tried to ease it by mentioning my own
lapses as I waded through items such as stripping our beds properly
(i.e. folding all the blankets separately), disposing of cigarette
ends, economizing on electricity, etc., etc. Dorcas's face was
livid and she exploded before I was half-way through. Alice also
felt very strongly, Tommy sat dumb and scared, while the other two
supported me a little. We talked heatedly till midnight (wasting
electricity) and some hard words passed. I was told I'd acted in an
extremely unprofessional way, whatever disgrace that might imply.
They then said they supposed I would report their remarks to Mrs
Strang. I said I would leave them to say what they wished; that I
would only report whatever they asked me to say. Initially they
suggested some very awkward things but, after Mrs Briggs intervened,
I was asked simply to report that 'the staff hadn't liked it'. Then
we calmed down a little, realizing we were in charge together and
had seen worse days in the past. Mrs Briggs had the last word,
saying she would keep her own countenance about any action she might
take.

43

Next morning to my further embarrassment, I was in charge of
Dorcas's classroom because she was not allowed to work over duty
hours. The main bright spot, which sent me into a cupboard for a
private laugh, was Josie's special study of Vertebrates. She took
half the morning to write: 'There is 2 kind of vertebrate, warm and
cold bloody. Fish is cold bloody.' (So are some of us, I thought.)
At break-time Mrs Hotchkiss called unexpectedly. (She was one of
the committee, dead now. She used a long cigarette-holder and Miss
Gracey once went to tea with her armed with an even longer
cigarette-holder saying, 'I'll scotch the Hotch with this!')

The following evening I went to meet the London train, and had a
gin on the platform while I waited. Then while I scanned the
passengers on arrival, a great voice called 'Sparrow, I've been
waiting five minutes'. On the return journey she enquired how the
staff-book-reading had gone. 'Oh,' I replied, 'the staff asked me
to tell you they hadn't liked it.' She tried hard to elicit more,
finally saying: 'When you get to know me better you'll know that I
can get anything out of anybody - I pester until I do.' I said,
rather desperately but basically confident of being on very good
terms with her, 'When you get to know me better you'll know that if
I decide not to speak wild horses won't make me.' Actually of
course I had never yet been put to the test, but she took this
fairly seriously and I have not been 'brainwashed' to the extent
suffered by some subsequent colleagues.

Back at Downcroft, she kept me in close attendance upon her,
burst into the staff-room where Dorcas almost ignored her, and
flounced out, making some comment to me about Dorcas which made the
staff think I'd 'turned'. I gave her a message from Mr Marsh, whom
she telephoned with unprovoked rudeness. Then she withdrew to her
rooms and I joined the staff. Mrs Briggs 'sat dummel', thinking us
'as free of manners as what a toad is of a feather' (her special
phrase); then, with a pink spot on both elderly cheeks, she said,
'I've never been afraid of a 'Eadmistress yet and I'm not going to
start now', and marched upstairs to Mrs Strang.

Next morning I was to go on a week's leave. (An old man was
temporarily farm assistant, but not for long because his earnings
affected his pension.) I disliked leaving with things as they were.
Mrs Strang was extremely cold towards me - apparently Mrs Briggs had
told her that the whole thing was upsetting for me. After breakfast
Mrs Hotchkiss telephoned; Mrs Briggs had told her the story and she
wished to see Mrs Strang about it immediately. Mrs Strang was quite
wild with rage and I remember the girls' white faces, imagining they
must be at fault. Dorcas finally handed in her notice that morning
and was due to leave in April. Alice also spoke her mind,
unhandicapped by any hole in her head. Mr Marsh drove me to the
station and I left with everything topsy-turvy, feeling to have
offended most people. Even he said he wanted to have a fatherly
talk with me on my return. 'Let's have it now!' I said crossly. He
said he thought I was trying to make trouble for him on the
garden - I assured him I wasn't and he believed me.

Things seemed to have calmed down when I returned. Mrs Strang
was rather more careful of us for a time. A sow farrowed overnight
the day I came back - the last two piglets were extremely weak,
unlikely to live, though I settled them in to the milk bar and left

them to take their chance (a real farmer might have knocked them on the head) and then I spent the morning asleep in bed. Just before lunch I found two farm-girls self-righteously nursing the weak piglets like babies, by the boiler-room fire. They had skived all morning, and risked the sow rejecting her weaklings, so I had to try to save them after the girls' moral blackmail. Mrs Strang was away overnight, so I took the two piglets to my bedroom, nestling in a box, plus hot water bottle and feeding bottle. They cried so much that I spent half the night on the staff-room sofa rather than disturb the dormitories either side my bedroom. I confessed a little nervously to Mrs Strang on her return, and found myself organized in sick bay for the second night. One piglet died during the night. The following evening three candidates were arriving for the Deputy's post - Mrs Strang said would I please tell her as soon as the second piglet died because it was disorganizing the sleeping arrangements for the visitors. It obligingly died at 7 p.m. and I buried it, feeling quite nauseated by the smell of sickly piglets, but that Mrs S had been sweetly accommodating in spite of her small tolerance for the indecision of death.

I think of the next phase as a time of general purge. Apart from the arrival of a new Deputy, a lively, feminine person with much relevant previous experience, called Miss Scott, we seemed largely to concentrate on getting rid of girls and animals. Cats were first to go. We had had a lot of cats and kittens. Homes were found for some, and Mrs S sorted out the remainder. I had to take the tabby kitten (the one she'd been so gentle with the first evening) to the vet to be destroyed. I also took Pip to be castrated and Freckles to be spayed. Dear old Freckles (who has changed now) did not give in easily, being a cat of character and the longest inmate here. Mrs S rang the vet in great indignation several weeks after the operation: 'The cat's copulating outside my office window at this moment.'

The rabbits were purged next. After the changeover, when they had belonged to individual girls, they were found to be in a dirty, unhealthy condition so I received all thirteen back to the farm and got them into shape again. In late March I happened to mention at lunch-time that one had died during an exceptionally cold night. Mrs S must have been in a bad mood (she had said already that there was no room for moods in the school apart from her own). She reacted amazingly by deciding all the rabbits must be destroyed. I said the girls would be very upset. She replied icily, 'Does that matter?' I said yes, I thought it did. She lost her temper, saying she had been very patient with us but in future was going to 'barge'. She rang a committee member for permission, and obtained agreement on condition that 'Miss Sparrow isn't upset about it'. The next question, she said, is 'Who will do it - Marsh or Evans?' I knew they would either refuse or muff it (though they did volunteer to dig a grave in frozen earth). I felt unable to face such unnecessary mass slaughter by myself so enlisted Mr Laycock's help. Mrs Strang told the girls the rabbits were going to be 'put to sleep because they are suffering from a disease'. Vanessa told me she would go berserk if Lynne's rabbit (the only black one) were killed. I said I'd mention this to Mrs Strang, but that if the rabbits had a disease it would probably be impossible to keep one.

This was just to prepare her - the rabbits were perfectly healthy. Later Mrs S asked whether I thought 'the men would like any rabbits?' I leapt at this, saying perhaps they would have all the rabbits, especially Lynne's. She said she meant to eat. Certainly not. We had several arguments during the afternoon, and I went into the office at tea-time where Mrs S and Mrs Pemberton were talking about someone awkward who argued, and I slowly realized this person was myself.

At supper-time, Mrs Strang thought it was all over and gushed a bit. But I was still full of apprehension, trying to eat. Mr Laycock arrived during supper and we went off with a torch to kill the twelve rabbits quickly with a stick. Later that evening it had been such a miserable day that I thought perhaps I had been awkward and that I should have managed my own department with less fuss. So, ridiculously, I apologized to Mrs Strang for arguing. She smiled artificially and replied, 'Don't worry, Sparrow, you won't do it again.' This was the last straw and suddenly I hoped I would. Suddenly I saw the real future danger as not having courage to argue enough. The following Sunday I was summoned to the office with Ann, who had been very fond of her rabbit. In her letter home that day she wrote frankly about the death leaving traces of blood on the ice rather than being a 'putting to sleep', and she composed a hymn, to the tune of 'Abide with Me', about meeting her rabbit in heaven. She was given a thorough dressing down in my presence, and I walked out too when she was dismissed. I took Mrs Strang's part about those wretched rabbits for about a week before I realized that it was I with whom the girls were angry. When I told them one sometimes had to do these things on a farm but that I'd hated doing it, they forgave me.

The next purge did not involve death but was almost more worrying. The departure of Dorcas could be included in it. When Miss Gracey was here we all gathered pleasantly to wave off anybody, girl or staff, who was leaving, but Dorcas seemed so isolated in comparison, partly with Mrs Strang refusing to speak to her, that I came over specially from the farm to say good-bye. A few girls from the kitchen and schoolroom also slipped out to wave after her taxi. Just after, when I was taking dinner with the girls, Mrs Strang entered and told all those who had gone out to wave to Miss Dorcas to stand up. They each lost 15 marks, ostensibly because the warning bell for dinner had not then rung. The loss of a mark at that stage meant the loss of a penny pocket money - my own salary was not penalized. Later in the year of purge, we had several 'mock transfers'.

Because the girls' behaviour was no longer quite so abnormally perfect, Mrs Strang periodically threatened them that there would be transfers, though I don't know why this was supposed to be such a terrible punishment. Then a girl would disappear exactly as though she were being transferred, but in fact secret arrangements had been made beforehand for her to return to her own home. Miss Scott and Mr Marsh were usually escorts, I was not directly involved nor were plans discussed with the staff. Once the trio reached the nearest big railway station, the girl's uniform was changed in the cloakroom to her 'disposal outfit', she was told she was actually going home, and was despatched on her own, in a complete daze I imagine. Then

Mrs Strang would say to the remaining girls, 'What did I tell you?'
She thought this honest, having gone through the motions of a
transfer without specifically stating it.

Seven girls disappeared in this way, including Pearl, though I
don't know where she went as she had no home elsewhere. Most were
ex-Gracey girls, regarded as bad blood. I did not like it at all.
Several of us thought it risky anyway. What if they had to come
back, or met current inmates on leave in London? In fact none
returned, except Pearl - the rest simply disappeared. Mrs Strang
carried it off with her usual luck though she pursued the policy
only briefly. The committee was probably unaware - they only know
our girls by report. I don't know how far the girls themselves
realize they have a better chance of leaving if they behave badly
than if they toe the line, though they are told the opposite in
general. I hate the way things often happen here for mere
expediency - it makes our work a complete farce. The system,
especially earlier, runs like clockwork and we sometimes forget
there would be no need to sweep and dust, dig and delve if the lives
of a large group of adolescents were not entrusted to our care.

Downcroft filled to capacity in a few months after Mrs Strang's
arrival, partly with recalls from the former régime, some of whom
were treated harshly. I remember Val being locked up alone in a
small dormitory for many days. It was my task to 'exercise her' on
the farm by herself during each lunch hour. However cold the
weather, she wore only underclothes and a cotton overall (as do all
the house-girls) so I used to put on an extra layer of top clothes
myself and lend the surplus to Val out of doors unseen. This had a
surreptitious flavour, which I feared Mrs Strang might regard in a
homosexual light, but I saw no alternative, and Val used my clothes
without a word passing at the time or after. We had virtually no
absconding and it was months before we needed to attend the VD
clinic. But when the time came, our GP told Mrs S that Miss Sparrow
would know the clinic times. I stated the times rather importantly
and took two girls to the hospital twenty miles away. As we sat in
the waiting room (where I was sometimes asked for my number) a
harassed male nurse asked to speak to me aside. 'It's Males!' he
said. 'What is males?' I asked. 'This is the males' clinic time,'
he said. The times had changed! We were smuggled quickly into
another waiting room although the present one was empty, the girls
quite unconscious of this being at all funny.

Easter Monday that year was an exceptionally happy day. We all
went out for a picnic to some woods. Miss Scott and Alice were in
fine form, and I paddled and pottered with the girls in a stream,
though Mrs Strang 'cleared up' the natural habitat with our help
before we left in a way which made Miss Scott swear under her
breath. After Easter I felt chronically tired, as there still
seemed to be no let up after the changeover as we had expected, so I
made a hasty request to the GP during his routine visit here for
something to 'pep me up', meaning a conventional tonic. I took the
first of the pills prescribed, hoping only for long-term effects but
felt a new woman almost immediately. Tommy said it was a miracle.
I was full of ideas, in and out of working hours, and had more than
enough energy to put them into practice.

A pore on the face of Britain was changed that summer as we

worked on the farm. I drew cartoons far into the night. Mrs Strang
got hold of the first by accident, enjoyed it and was constantly
demanding them, sometimes to send to inspectors to demonstrate our
happy state. She (also most staff and some girls) is an ideal
'cartoon subject' and in those days I had no qualms in drawing her
fairly true to life, teasing her about many of her 'funny little
ways'. She always shouted with laughter at these drawings and kept
a book of them (nowadays I draw her rarely, or a thinner nondescript
backview if at all). In fact I found a cartoon was the best way of
making a point without offending her. For instance, though I often
need to go over to the farm during the night on my own initiative,
she not infrequently woke me to investigate trouble which usually
turned out to be non-existent - a bellowing cow would prove to
belong to a neighbouring farm. So I drew a picture of our cows on
their hindlegs demonstrating with rebellious placards in the
dark - she took the hint that this was unlikely to happen and
stopped waking me at night.
    The word placard reminds me of a shameful action of mine. A new
junior, Angela, very gawky and dim, was an extreme irritant to Mrs
Strang through her continual seeking for attention. Mrs Strang
asked me to make a placard inscribed 'PLEASE NOTICE ME' for Angela
to wear. I find it hard to believe that I did so without question,
and can only plead my enjoyment of making things. Whatever else,
the finished placard was beautifully painted in black lettering on
white plywood. It was only as I was in the act of delivering it to
Mrs Strang's office that I realized its enormity. I clapped it down
on her desk. 'What is the matter, Sparrow?' 'It reeks of David
Copperfield.' 'Whatever are you saying, child?' 'The placard he
wore at school about biting...', quite incoherent. She explained
that I must not credit Angela with my own sensitivity, that it is my
weakness to imagine the girls have feelings such as I might have. I
had never thought of myself as 'sensitive', but certainly felt too
sensitive to discuss the question, so withdrew embarrassed. Angela
wore the placard for quite a time - I forget whether for days or
weeks, but can only hope it brought her a little nice attention.
    I am also uncomfortable about the 'religious' siftings and
judgments on the girls. Mrs Strang is strongly non-conformist (i.e.
in denomination) and a lay preacher to boot, but, as with sex, we
seem to stress its least attractive side. Girls who wish to be
confirmed often seem to fall by the wayside and have to face sarcasm
about their noble intentions. One evening while I was on dormitory-
duty, Pat confided that she very much wanted to be confirmed, had
thought a lot about it, and could I advise her how to tell Mrs
Strang this? (Girls quite often ask us how best to phrase requests.
One tries, knowing it may well prove unacceptable anyway, and that
Mrs S will be annoyed if she senses tactful interference in the
background.) I advised Pat to tell Mrs Strang when she was not
'busy' - our euphemism for a bad mood - and to put it just as she
had told me. Pat said, 'I shan't be able to do it without beating
round the bush.' I said, 'I think Mrs Strang would rather you came
straight to the point - then you'll just have to see how the
conversation follows on. Anyway there's no doubt God will have a
warm welcome for you.' We were talking with our backs to the open
bathroom door. I suddenly swung round, sensing a Presence, and

there was Mrs Strang, looking hoity-toity. Pat was despatched
promptly with flea-ridden ears, and it was some weeks before she
ventured to re-open the subject. I tried to mollify Mrs S on her
behalf, without success.

It is often my responsibility to take the communicants to church.
Mrs Strang, in handing them over to me might say, 'Here's your
group, Miss Sparrow. LOOK AT THEM! A nice little lot! Call
themselves communicants...', while I smile uncertainly. We seem
fairly catholic, if narrow-minded otherwise, in our range of
'worship'. The girls occasionally went to 'Youth for Christ'
meetings in Glebe - this was perhaps regarded as an outing rather
than a chance for evangelical conversion, which none of us saw as
desirable. I was a bit concerned about the girls going, and being
extra burdened about their 'sin' as they do naturally feel despised
by the world already. One evening two inexperienced members of
staff took the school to such a meeting, where there must have been
a most moving speaker. The whole school, except two hardened
sinners, insisted on going up to be saved. My two colleagues were
torn between embarrassed reluctance and doing their duty, but had to
join in the mass repentance and salvation. Then they returned to
confess on a lower plane. Mrs Strang was horrified, talked to the
school privately, and individual girls were twitted about their
false piety when next they slipped up. We stopped attending these
particular functions - just as well, I thought, if the girls were to
be subjected to such emotional pressures but refused the outlet.

The girls are absurdly grateful for any little treat, which often
ends with a blast. Once I accompanied them to a dullish missionary
meeting, and on the way home they said how lovely it had been. Some
of them had not been out for weeks and, knowing what sort of
amusement they would naturally have chosen, I felt we were no longer
on this earth, so said I had found the meeting a bit dull, and they
secretly agreed. Some people have the gift of giving a magic spark
to the most ordinary proceedings, and some people destroy what spark
exists from occasions which sound pleasant on paper. I was happy
because I love the work and the place, and have plenty of fun in odd
moments. (Two of my private games are 'poor man's polo', which
requires skill in posting a letter in a wall pillar box on one's
right hand side without stopping the car, and clergy-chasing on
railway journeys. This started when I happened to travel with a
bishop, followed by a vicar's widow on one journey, and thereafter I
play at finding some clerical, monk or nun-like garb on the
platform, following it into the carriage, full of inward mirth,
thinking it might be a nice change for them to be actively sought
even if unawares.) But what life here must be like for the girls!
In those early days especially it was slog, slog, day in day out,
with the main excitement provided when somebody other than their
individual selves is in trouble.

Once when Miss Scott saw me dressed for evening church, she said
it was all wrong that a girl of my age should be shut away from the
world. Mrs Strang disagreed sourly: 'Sparrow's sown her wild oats.'
I murmured, 'I thought oats were for men but if women are included
I've still got a few in reserve.' For about the first year it was
my frequent duty to take the girls who need to work on Sunday
morning to an evening service at the Baptist chapel. It was a rush

for me to change from farm clothes to chapel clothes, and one
particular Sunday Mrs Strang made it more of a rush than usual so
that I had no time to wash properly after calving a cow. She asked
me if I felt 'cold round the legs' (without breeches) as I snatched
a sandwich from the staff tea-trolley just before setting off for
chapel. 'No,' I replied, fairly good humouredly, 'I feel hot round
the collar.' She took this as rudeness and I was thereafter removed
from regular chapel rota. Her reactions, even when on good terms
with one, tend to be unpredictable. For instance, the staff were
discussing Judo once in our free time, although Miss Scott squealed
before I had a chance to demonstrate my one hold but she said
jokingly to Mrs Strang later (who is twice my size) that she had
better watch out with a Judo expert in the camp. To our embarrassment the joke misfired: 'You try anything like that with me, young
lady, and you'll be very sorry for yourself by the time I've
finished with you!'

    'Prayers' within the school are often as strange as in the former
era. Sometimes the girls are given a severe telling off, and then
commanded 'to sing "Now Thank we all our God", whether you are
thankful or not'. Mrs Strang uses a special book of very talkative
prayers, designed to cover all possible life events. I quite like
them, except that she tends to read some bits very significantly to
fit any member temporarily out of favour. Mr Marsh stopped
attending prayers after he, recently having crossed swords and lost,
was singled out as follows: 'If any be sulking here, let it be day
about that person, so that he shall see himself as he is, and be
ashamed.' The poor man is still sore about 'if any be sulking
here'. In the early days we had a little ceremony of the 'mid-week
knicker change' and the classic time was when Mrs Strang pronounced
the blessing without taking breath in between: 'The blessing of God
Almighty ... with us all, now and always, Amen Knickers off.' In
this place one is often torn inwardly between laughter and tears.

    Summing up this semi-religious section, I would say our girls are
most impressed when church or chapel members are openly friendly and
treat them as ordinary human beings. They do try to take in all the
different things they are told. I remember Diane being very upset
when her grandmother died. She suddenly realized she would
ultimately die herself - 'And what's more, Miss Sparrow, I heard
this morning that there's no eternal life - Miss Thomas told
me - she says the kingdom of heaven's in this world.' She was very
willing to believe it might possibly be in both worlds, and went off
more comfortably.

CHAPTER 8

If other people's sensitivity and religious fervour cannot be measured, neither can their bladders and, until there is some way of knowing, I shall continue to let girls go to the lavatory when they ask. There are strict rules about it here as though they were machines. No girl is allowed to go during our rare visits to the cinema - this is made clear to everybody beforehand. But the staff are not told what to do if a girl simply cannot wait, except that such a girl will never be allowed to go to the pictures again. What with the strain of thinking about it or the excitement of the film, I have seen girls crying in their dilemma or shamming ill in order to be allowed to go out. Occasionally they wet the seats in the picture-house, though fortunately we are too numerous a potential audience for the manager to complain. If any girl has wet pants, Mrs Strang knows swiftly by a particular one of her six senses and the girl is often publicly humiliated about it, if she is not already hardened by necessity.

   For the most part, instead of going out to the cinema, we have our own projector for films on winter Saturday evenings - with poor sound at first, and sometimes with a few girls sitting in reverse from the screen for punishment. When we do go out anywhere, our exact Ps and Qs are detailed beforehand, everyone knows in advance where to sit, and which 'naughty' girls on either side of a specified member of staff. Once there, having made a slight exhibition of ourselves while settling according to orders, we then tend to behave better than anyone else. In their free time in the common-room, there are clear rules: voices must be low, certain girls must not sit together, everyone must DO something (read, knit, sew, etc.) and I believe the member of staff on duty is supposed to keep an ear on conversation to see that none of numerous banned topics arise. Table tennis proved 'too noisy'. As the staff conversation also becomes increasingly regulated, it is fortunate that the weather gives us constant surprises. The girls shop little except on the time table. Needs are met in a dull, mass-produced manner. Instead of each girl buying her own sticky bag of sweets, a large tin of toffees is rationed out.

   But it was a long time before I became painfully aware of the soul-destroying nature of our totally changed way of life. To start

with it seemed comparatively peaceful, with more scope for private
enjoyment in one's free time in the outside world. What influenced
me most, and prevented my seeing my fellows' discomfort often, was
the fact that Mrs Strang made a great favourite of me and generally
did her utmost to smooth my path. And yet I slowly discovered that
her highly-organized smoothings tend to cause extra complications.
To give only two examples: I once said entirely as a joke that to
have a hammock on the farm would simplify my nocturnal visitations
for animals' illness and confinements. That very day a local firm
fetched a string hammock from a city thirty miles away and fixed up
two sets of screws, in the piggery and in a calving-box. So on the
first possible occasion, in late May, I felt compelled to sleep on
the farm, and settled myself about 10.30 p.m. in the piggery with
two grey blankets and my unloaded air pistol in case of snoopers.
Once was enough - the sow was ready to farrow but did not begin
until breakfast-time, there were rats, it was cold, I fell out of
the hammock, the goats nearly died of curiosity, and there was a
surprising amount of restless night life. I crept back to my own
bed at 5 a.m., and have never used the hammock since, even though
Mrs Strang is displeased. Later on, I sometimes go dizzy in the
night, and feel quite sea-sick to imagine dizziness in a hammock.
    The second of many examples involved Hat-trick, our silliest cow,
who was made a fool of in calfhood and is awkward to handle full-
grown. Late one winter night I found her in great pain, probably
with colic, so I gave her a strong drench, and a second quickly
during the night, and she seemed back to normal next morning. But I
rang the vet, saying I would like him to visit within the next few
days, because it was proving difficult to get Hat-trick into calf
and there were two or three other minor things requiring advice.
The vet (partner to my usual one, who knows my ordinary ability)
rang Mrs Strang's office during the morning to say he would come
two days hence. She said he must come immediately; that the cow was
in agony and I had 'been up all night'. The first I knew of it was
when he turned up an hour later, though extremely busy, asking if
the cow was still alive. Hat-trick looked the picture of health. I
apologized, explaining that a headmistress in this type of school
has to be in the habit of making forceful decisions. He was angry,
but said he would examine Hat-trick for her apparent infertility.
His verdict was: 'All I can prescribe is a sedative for your
headmistress.' As discussion went on, I felt he was being too
irritable so, when he asked 'Is she having regular periods?' I
retaliated by replying 'Do you mean the cow or the headmistress?'
(In fact this might have been part of the latter's trouble.
Certainly her wild tempers in the early years were worse than we
experience nowadays. Often she seemed to lose all self-control,
especially when overtired, but was always touchingly penitent by
next day.)
    Mrs Strang is absurdly sensitive herself and quick to take a
hint - often before one is intended. But why, I used to wonder, if
she was so easily hurt herself, did she trample roughshod over many
other people's feelings? Considering she is such 'a strong
character', she surprisingly often seems pathetic, and any time I
have felt to have a slight upper hand - when driven to it by
desperation - I have almost immediately relinquished it (certainly

within two days) through being sorry for her. Then she usually
walks in with force and pays one back at a high rate of interest. I
only slowly saw her pattern, but even now I have seen it for nearly
three years I am still a sitting duck. Looking back, I would say I
was the most loyal member of staff during her first eighteen months,
though I have stopped using the word loyalty. Miss Scott, initially
a great asset with a keen sense of fun, gradually became waspish and
seemed set on making trouble for Mrs Strang. I think one reason for
the latter's early cultivation of me was that she must always have
expected a show-down amongst the staff, and perhaps thought I would
influence my colleagues in her direction. She saw me as the most
popular member of staff, as the staff's 'white-haired boy'.
Actually of course the staff all have minds of their own, even if
not exactly free to use their individual personalities and gifts.
    That summer of 19X6 we were again without a teacher (after Dorcas
went) for a long time. I often had most of the school working on
the farm, and Mrs Strang (formidable in a boiler-suit, with sledge-
hammer and bush-saw) did a great deal of work outside. Mr Marsh
sensibly kept her out of his garden but she got her foot in on the
farm. We tackled numerous large-scale jobs and moved mountains
which might have been better left where nature placed them. For
instance, she cut down three spinneys, I pulled out the stumps with
the hydraulic lift on the tractor, we moved the railings from these
attractive spinneys - the whole school lifting the railings wholesale, dragging them over to the farm, then each girl would dig a
hole and we would insert the railings afresh in one half-day (not
looking so nice when circular railings are re-set in a straight line
by a lot of females). We did many other jobs on this scale. For a
woman, Mrs Strang is amazingly handy with tools, but she will never
have the first idea about farming, or synchronize with the seasons.
She is extremely quick, far more so than I am, but her work does not
always last and needs constant repair, which I have to do privately
as she would be offended otherwise.
    My extraordinary energy came to an abrupt end in mid-summer when
the GP visited the farm one day, asked after my pills (not knowing
his partner had given me a second box) and I discovered my
miraculous tonic was actually Benzedrine. A great mistake, on my
part and his, and the aftermath was a sorry privation. I kept the
very last pill for the day of Mr Dean's visit - the farms and
gardens inspector - in order to be on top form. He was delighted by
the farm, so much so that he suggested ambitious plans for extension
over a period of three years, with an unrealistic increase of
livestock, crops and profits. As soon as he had gone, Mrs Strang
thumped me on the back, and said, 'Come on, let's go and see where
to put the new pig runs.' I felt overwhelmed and, after she had
heaved me unexpectedly over a locked gate when I'd taken enough
spring to get myself over, so that I fell heavily the other side, I
felt unable to be rushed and pushed any more, and told her about the
Benzedrine. She was a little annoyed not to have guessed, and
prescribed some more pills (with an arsenical content) as antidote,
but I decided privately to recover slowly by my own methods. I had
recently bought my first car for £80, an ancient drop-head coupé
with red wheels, which enabled more relaxed freedom. Also for the
first time I had a full-time farm assistant called Miss Groves, a

strong young girl, who was appointed to be 'brawn' complementing my 'brain'.

We had a system of marks then which became unmanageable by late summer 19X6 due to inflation. We had to deduct marks, at a loss of a penny per mark, for numerous trivial things. As girls have so little pocket money, I started by taking off no more than one or two marks. Gradually amounts crept up until, when I discovered Kim endangering another girl on a ladder she was supposed to be supporting, I took off twenty marks. Kim by now was Head Girl, Vanessa having been transferred elsewhere as beyond our help when she was found to be inciting her peers to rebellion. Mrs Strang scrutinized the mark book: 'Twenty marks off for shaking a ladder, Miss Sparrow? Twenty? Two hundred, more like!' That meant 16s 8d. Soon afterwards, for more trouble on the farm, Mrs Strang deducted a further 2,000 marks and put Kim in detention. When Kim incurred the impossible debt of at least 2,200d, that particular marks system finished, bankrupt.

(In this version of my diary, I may seem to be writing disproportionately much about the Heads and myself, but of course one's fate rather hangs upon the Head, and I do not want to say overmuch about my enjoyable colleagues, whose discomforts in any case are fairly similar to mine.) Mrs Strang occasionally tells the girls how fortunate they are in having a well-qualified staff. One girl wrote home: 'We have the best quality staff here.' Mrs S sometimes tells people, even the girls, what a state the staff were in when she took over. She says we were black and blue, which is far from true. We might have been covered in bruises, scratches and bites if the Gracey era's accretions had been cumulative, but these outward scars recover quickly and are never very noticeable on one person at any one moment. Mrs Strang felt safe enough to laugh at herself occasionally in her first year here. We were invited to laugh when a parent wrote to her daughter, 'do as Mrs Strang tells you, she is so sweet and patient', but, having laughed, we found it was only the 'sweet' which was supposed to be funny. It makes her angry when any of the staff or girls show concern for someone in difficulties. One evening, during my Benzedrine aftermath, colleagues must have told her I looked tired and ill. I was semi-off duty the following day, and had planned a lazy, pleasant day for myself with plenty of sleep. I was fast asleep when she burst into my bedroom like a thunder-clap at 8.15 a.m., saying the staff had been complaining about me and 'I'm the last to be told, as usual', and that if I so much as moved from bed all day she would smack me. I was annoyed at this unnecessarily rude awakening and snapped, 'You'll do no such thing!' and she flounced out again, leaving me angry, shaken, with all feeling of sleep gone. Similarly, on several occasions, committee members or inspectors told her I looked 'tense', and I, after instruction, would be coaxed forward on their next visit to explain that my appearance is misleading. I have gradually begun to see a little that even her anger, which is literally dreadful, is a mark of her own concern sometimes, and in between bouts she can be remarkably considerate.

Very rarely do we have an incident reminiscent of the Gracey era. So I quite enjoyed one this summer of 19X6. Rosie, usually quiet, the one who jumped on a policeman's back in the 'riot', was like a

great cave-woman, with legs like tree-trunks and rare primitive
rages. Now she was working as domestic help on a farm about ten
miles away. Her employer, Mrs Crayford, had a series of our girls,
and I have collected several loads of dirty clothes of girls who
have gone adrift there, with Mrs Crayford moaning alongside, 'And
I've been so good to her, Miss Sparrow.' On this particular
afternoon, I drove Miss Scott there because Rosie was being
difficult, and I waited outside in the van. Very soon Rosie ran out
of the house, down the road. Miss Scott emerged and made this
classic remark: 'You go after her, I don't want to make a scene in
the road.' I ran and ran, across a ploughed field in good clothes,
and found Rosie at the far end like an elephant at bay. She had
lost a shoe in boggy ground and was stuck on the farther side of a
barbed wire fence. I reached her too breathless to speak and weak
with suppressed laughter, having just been reading a modern fairy
story in which the heroine found it worked when she said to someone,
'Be a wood-louse', and having an impulse to try this magic on
formidable Rosie. I freed her from the wire, and gave her her lost
shoe, foolishly thinking she would come with me because I had helped
her. She snatched her shoe, felled me with a look, and ran on
through a row of back gardens. I returned to consult with Miss
Scott, and we with Mrs Crayford pursued Rosie in the van. We
spotted her in some vast woods. Apparently Miss Scott was also
averse to making a scene in the woods. I glanced round after Mrs
Crayford had pushed me over a ditch with unnecessary ardour, and saw
Miss Scott swaying with laughter in the lane. Mrs Crayford and I
struggled through undergrowth, the former talking hysterically.
'But I've been so good to her, Miss Sparrow....Haven't I been good
to you, Rosie?' she called out. Loud, but far off, came the answer:
'NO!' We gave up after a time and Rosie returned quietly with the
police later that day.
    Some time in autumn 19X6, Miss Scott tackled me. She was
thinking of complaining to the committee about the girls being
overworked out-of-doors, and asked whether I would support her. I
hesitated before refusing, saying I wanted 'to do the right thing,
but...'; that I had driven the girls hard myself that summer, and I
still felt the present Head's leadership was preferable. Miss Scott
said, 'You're not here to feather your own nest, you know.' (It was
truly better feathered than others still, and they may have slightly
resented the preferential treatment I once received.) Meanwhile
Miss Crandle warned Mrs Strang on her own initiative about Miss
Scott's growing mistrust of the régime. Mrs Strang tried to involve
me, asking 'What shall we do?' I felt she need do nothing except
watch her step, and that she was quite capable of knowing what best
to do.
    Kim, having crashed from the Head Girl's pedestal, absconded in
September with another girl, and we did not see them again. She was
timid in both régimes, but a keen Head Girl temporarily - for
example, giving Mrs Strang a list of girls who had not hung their
cardigans up by the tabs ('I thought you'd like to know after being
so good giving them to us') and reporting that a fellow prefect had
been trying to get into another girl's bed, and that she, Kim, had
snooped outside the dormitory door night after night to gain this
information. However, by now, she must have been terrified of

returning to Downcroft, and made a long statement to the police.
Mrs Strang burst into my bedroom with the news when I was off duty,
saying copies of the statement had been sent to our committee and
inspectorate. The telephone rang again; she answered it and
returned to say it was the chairman again (Mr French) advising her
on no account to tell her staff. 'Anyway, I've told you now,' she
said, and continued discussion, very het-up.

I thought, at the time, from my limited direct observations, that
about half Kim's allegations were true. I had already offered to
help if I could at all, and was just going to say which parts of the
statement I considered true and which false, when Mrs Strang said,
'And you know I've never laid hands on Kim,' which made me speechless because I had seen her slap Kim's face three times - only a
fraction of the 'evidence'. She perceived my doubts, thanked me for
my promise of help, and departed hastily. By now, realizing she
intended to deny the whole thing, I could have kicked myself for
offering support. In the event, we heard little more. The
committee met, and Miss Merton visited specially, but Mrs Strang
must have cleared herself without my assistance.

All I heard, via Mr Marsh, was that one of his garden prefects
had told him (so it may not be true, though it has a Strangian ring
about it) that 'Any girl not looking cheerful during Miss Merton's
visit will have another six months put on her time.' I was supposed
to be available for the chairman's visit, but mercifully he came
early while I was out for a jaunt. Mrs Strang sent for me after,
looking as though she had been crying; she had told Mr French, she
said, that he (as boss of a large firm) would know what a lonely
position the Head's is, but that he has a wife to go home to....

Our first November the 5th in this reign was a great contrast.
We stood in sorted ranks, with staff stationed on the flanks and
rear, while Miss Scott and Mr Marsh let off a small, slow string of
fireworks fifty yards away. The only entertaining aspect was that
the squibs seemed damp. We have never celebrated Guy Fawkes Day
since, though the idea of gun-powder in our cellars becomes
increasingly tempting. Mrs Strang was touchingly keen for us to
mark the completion of her first year here in early December. Once,
that autumn, while the Head was on leave, the girls were quite
difficult, and when things grew almost out of hand on a Saturday
morning, Miss Scott (full of grit, though often fish-wifey by now)
said she would look after the girls entirely by herself and have
them 'on silence' the whole weekend. They were accustomed to this
for short periods during meal-times, but I felt such prolonged
silence was as dangerously explosive as it was unsuitable ethically.
I feel almost sure Mrs Strang knew of this 'weekend of silence' on
her return, and that she did not question it at the time.

Just before Christmas 19X6, Mrs de Villiers (a committee member,
always friendly to me, though seriously ill now) took Mrs Strang and
me - saying 'dear little Sparrow' as we set off - to some farming
friends of hers to buy a new pedigree cow. I chose a nice little
cow, whom the girls re-christened Holly, and whose character and
milk yield have developed well since coming to us. We had tea with
Mrs de Villiers at her home. After tea she asked Mrs Strang to go
and play the grand piano to us in another room, and she took this
opportunity to ask me whether I thought Mrs Strang is 'too hard on

the girls' (after Kim, I suppose). I felt awkward while Mrs S was
playing innocently from afar, and said I thought she has a tough
exterior but is gentle underneath (she was then usually to me, which
inevitably influences one's opinion) and that I prefer people not to
have all their good qualities on the surface! Mrs de Villiers
looked non-committal, and later thanked Mrs Strang charmingly for
her brief recital, though I heard few notes of music myself in the
circumstances. Then I drove Mrs S several miles back here,
beginning to appreciate more why Dorcas described me as amoral.

I think that was the last time I was actually asked to give my
opinion of Mrs Strang to outside officials. I feel all the more
reluctant to take action now, because of the contrast with my early
'loyalty'. Officials can hardly help being puzzled. But I defy any
young person, not yet bitten by this sort of thing, to have even the
beginnings of a clear picture of Mrs Strang until they have
experienced it over a period of time. Part of my trouble is that I
have too much innate respect for authority, and have taken for
granted since childhood (without being disillusioned until Downcroft
days) that all headmistresses are pillars of integrity, far above
reproach. In some ways the girls are more quaintly grown up than
we are - for instance, Hazard, the most temperamental cow, went
through a minor kicking phase and Shirley, who usually hand-milked
her, became frightened. I took over for a few days until Hazard had
quietened, then gave her back to Shirley, asking whether she might
feel any more confident now if Hazard became fidgety again? 'I
think I'd just overlook it,' Shirley said, 'after all, she is a dumb
beast!'

If Mrs Strang has good qualities, on or below the surface, I had
better think what they are quickly. A lot of them go both ways: her
enthusiasm and energy, her potential gentleness and kindness and
ability to deal with illness, her unsureness, her knowledge (?) of
people and understanding (?) of the girls, her personal magnetism
and ability to inspire affection out of heaven knows what, her
organizing powers (?) and leadership, her pathos and humility in
needing praise, her practical mind, her 'sense of humour' and the
fact that she does not exactly get on one's nerves (because of being
short and sharp). There may be more things. In the next world,
without her gastric trouble and awkward temperament and most of all
her fears, she might be very nice to know, though I shall not seek
her out.

Christmas 19X6 was quiet but pleasant on the whole. Mrs Strang
gave the staff her usual Christmas present of a bottle of
sherry - our main official annual drink - this year inscribed with
'Best wishes and thanks for your loyalty'. It gave none of us
hiccups. But in fact Sparrow, not an early bird, was nearer worm-
turning than she knew.

CHAPTER 9

New Year's Eve - our one and only Strangian 'celebration' - was most
odd. We slept in the evening, had an enormous supper about 10.30
and then listened to a church service on the radio in the common-
room, which was unusually chilly and cheerless. The girls sat
forlorn and sniffing with home-sickness on rows of chairs. Mrs
Strang sat on the platform, out of humour, full of cold; she goes in
for a cold in a big way, and trumpets daily when blowing her nose.
On the stroke of twelve we stood, uncertain whether we were meant to
pray or clap or greet each other. In the midst of this gloomy
scene, loud dance music broke out. We were organized into a little
dancing which ended disastrously - I think because Mrs Strang's
dancing evoked a bawdy remark from one of the girls. We just
managed to sing 'Auld Lang Syne'. Mrs Briggs, no doubt recalling
happier occasions here years ago, called out in a quavering old
voice that she would like to wish us all a very Happy New Year.
    Early in January 19X7, I was just thinking how surprisingly
healthy the staff are, when several fell ill with 'flu. We had a
new teacher in Dorcas's place now, Miss Palethorpe - old-fashioned
without being very old, a correct but perhaps uninspiring teacher,
and either surly or shy. Often her only contribution to conversation at meal-times was a loud belch which we were all too polite to
notice. One morning on my day off, Miss Scott (convalescing from
'flu) came to my room and said she must get outside before she went
mad. We arranged to go out for dinner that evening - Mrs Strang
became uneasy on hearing the plan. I went downstairs for lunch, and
found that my assistant had reported slight trouble on the farm to
Mrs Strang. As a result, Dot, one of the most capable girls, had
been taken off the farm. Then it had been decided that Josie, the
other most capable, was 'really at the bottom of it' so she was
taken off instead. I could not argue with Mrs Strang in front of
Josie, but I was upset. When Mrs S asked me to agree that Josie's
work was now poor, I said weakly and untruthfully that perhaps it
was not quite so good as it had been. Josie was given the daily job
of shifting coal and coke around the house. In the afternoon I went
out, and passed Josie with her wheelbarrow. I felt I must say
something to her, without undermining the Head's authority, so said
she would just have to take this punishment, even if it seemed

unfair, and that I was keen to have her back on the farm as soon as possible. She just looked bleakly at me.

In the evening, Miss Scott and I returned early from our jaunt and found Mrs Strang agitato. Josie had absconded; Mrs S had awaited my return thinking she might be hiding martyredly on the farm. Josie was reputed to have a very hot temper; a big, strong girl. Mrs Strang and I looked round the grounds and farm in thin snow. In one of the farm buildings, Josie popped up from behind the root-slicer, wearing my old raincoat (which I should not have left about). I said, 'Come along, Josie', briskly enough to satisfy Mrs S. She in turn spoke sentimentally, using the nick-name of Jo, and I realized that she (quite unlike Miss Gracey) was afraid of a fight. Josie screamed defiance and ran past us. Mrs S signalled me to follow her. I ran down the paths, about half a step behind, explaining as we went that things must seem very bad to her, but it was not yet beyond hope, and that I would help, if only..., etc. We ran round the back of the house and I wondered how much further, but she ran in through the back door and went to ground under a wash-basin.

After a few minutes she agreed to come to the office, and we met Mrs Strang there, who was different now re-inforcements were available. Josie walked quietly into detention. Then, at about 10.15, I went to Mrs Strang's room, and told her Josie did not deserve to come off the farm; that it was untrue for me to say her work had deteriorated. (It is extremely delicate to intervene on such occasions. It often means prolonged rather than briefer punishment for the girl - even, in an extremely clever way, that the girl is made to believe you have double-crossed her, and the end result is worse than the beginning.) In this case I carried it off to some extent, because Mrs S was feeling to need my support over Miss Scott, but my relationship with Josie was affected adversely in small ways later. I knew Josie would accept a stiff short-term punishment so long as she was allowed to return to the farm soon. Mrs Strang was going away on holiday the next day, so I suggested that Josie be kept on 'coke and coal' for the fortnight and be told she could come back to the farm if Mrs Strang received a good report of her on return. (This is what happened, and Josie amazed Miss Crandle by the ardour with which she shifted fuel.) I put this suggestion as tactfully as possible to Mrs S, but she went soft and dejected, saying perhaps she ought to resign from her post. This was off the immediate point, and I did not know what to say, and felt there had been enough emotional scenes during one 'day off', starting with Miss Scott in the morning, so I gradually eased myself out of the room, stepping backwards as from royalty. A few minutes later she came to my bedroom, and said should we go to see Josie; we went in our dressing-gowns - Mrs S went into detention to say good-night, and something about 'doing better in the morning' while I waited outside.

Mrs Strang had been steadily 'working up' on Miss Scott. I did not know then, but know the pattern now. Soon after her return from leave, she sent for me, saying the question of Miss Scott would come up at the next committee meeting, so would I be willing to speak (on Mrs Strang's side) if necessary. I heard myself replying rather piously and quite unpremeditatedly that I didn't want to be

connected with anything that wasn't 'above-board'! The effect on
Mrs Strang was startling - she went like a stone: 'As far as I know
I am absolutely straight in my dealings with everybody.' So we left
it at that. Two days later, the tension between Head and Deputy
exploded over a trivial matter of keys, and Miss Scott said she was
not being given her rightful place as Deputy (Miss Crandle being
even more efficient than she in the house). Mrs Strang marched into
the staff-room: 'I would just like to know where I stand - are you
with me or are you not?' We replied in awe that we were with her.
She said she intended to see the chairman next morning; that I was
to chauffer her and ensure that everything was 'above-board'.
    Poor Mr French seemed embarrassed. Mrs Strang caused me to see
him alone first for a few minutes, when I concentrated on saying
anything possible in favour of Mrs S rather than anything against
Miss S. Then Mrs Strang joined us, appearing pitifully weak. I
don't know that it was all 'above-board' but of course this peculiar
term made me wince by now while it back-fired on me. It seemed that
Miss Scott had made several criticisms of the staff, some of which
surprised us, though these may have been invented in order to
ferment our 'loyalty' to Mrs Strang. Mr French came to Downcroft
the same afternoon. The Head Girl, white-faced and breathless, ran
to fetch me urgently from the farm, and I came in to find Mrs Strang
in a greater state than I think I have ever seen her - 'like a wild
thing', one colleague said. The girls were terrified. She said she
would take over all the girls; would I collect all the staff because
Mr French wanted to see us. Apparently Miss Scott had been so
convincing, though saying little beyond 'I don't agree', and so sure
of our support, that Mrs Strang feared we had double-crossed her.
Mr French was a quiet, sane contrast, simply asking us whether in
our opinion Miss Scott had been given 'her rightful place as
Deputy'. We simply said yes, we thought so. It must of course be
difficult for the Deputy herself to know what her position is,
sandwiched between Head and staff.
    Soon after Mr French had gone, Miss Scott came in, looking very
strained and said sarcastically, 'Thank you ladies, thank you very
much.' Mrs Strang then replaced her, saying 'Thank you very much,
ladies,' more compos mentis. But their accidental use of virtually
the same phrase was bewildering, especially as it was now clear that
one of them would have to leave. My immediate aim was to avoid Mrs
Strang's own dismissal, something I still thought happened fairly
easily then. Later that evening, Mrs S told me, that if the staff
wished to help, our best plan would be to write a joint letter to
the committee. Four of us met in Alice's room after lights-out to
compose a letter. I am embarrassed to remember how I chaired that
situation, particularly when the Misses Palethorpe and Crandle are
subsequently such big wigs. Alice kept saying, 'Eh, Birdy, you do
remind me of meself when young!' They made one or two alterations
to my rough introductory paragraph; then Miss Palethorpe spoke for
almost the first time, saying the letter was adequate as it stood
(its main point being our gratitude for Mrs Strang's initial
'clearing up' here) and we were surprised to find she was right. I
typed the letter, eight residential members signed it, and we
received a polite, non-committal reply from Mr French in due course.
    In the meantime, I admired the way in which Miss Scott continued

quietly with her work, keeping up appearances. I felt very torn
about her, and had got across her less than other colleagues with my
working largely outdoors. But two days later she felt ill, had a
stiff neck, and was told to go off duty. She was in bed for a week,
seeing almost no one, except Alice, who became a kind of Switzerland
between Head and Deputy, and tended her kindly. Mrs Strang visited
once daily, never without a chaperone, and drew her own doctor into
the situation. I realized in an unexpected flash how the doctor
might be used. Fortunately doctors have plenty of integrity and
this one refused to commit himself further than that Miss Scott
needed rest. So she went off on sick leave. She and Alice had a
convalescent stroll round the farm the day before she left, and we
talked, about nothing, for a few minutes. Miss Scott looked frail,
much older, but not lacking in spirit. Alice took her to London,
half-way on her journey, and returned: 'It was ever so sad, Birdy,
I had to have a brandy afterwards' - most unlike her.
   On Alice's return, we had crumpets for tea, by a large log-fire,
creating the impression of a big happy family, but this is just when
we stopped (except among the lower staff). Alice's brief period of
being valued ceased abruptly and she slipped back philosophically
into the 'dog-house' or 'bad books' - our set terms for being out of
favour. Alice never got on very well with the Foreman, the Pope or
Queen Tip-toes, as Mrs Strang was variously called behind her back.
(Initially, Mrs Strang asked Alice, as cook, to keep her 'up to
scratch' on her diet, so when she asked for Christmas cake one mid-
morning, Alice replied gently: 'Are you sure you should?' 'I am
the headmistress of this school, and when I ask for Christmas cake,
I want CHRISTMAS CAKE!') Negotiations about Miss Scott continued
secretly for some weeks. Apparently the committee was reluctant to
dismiss her but hoped she would resign. She adamantly refused. Mrs
Percy was reported to have said, 'This nettle must be grasped.'
Then suddenly the 'weekend of silence' was recalled; Mrs Strang
expressed shocked surprise, though I am almost certain she knew of
it at the time, but now saw it could be used as evidence. Two
colleagues other than myself were required to confirm this and it
seemed finally to cook Miss Scott's goose. I felt uneasily that Mrs
S herself would have cooked much more quickly from this angle. Some
days later she announced jubilantly, 'Scott's resigned.' Again some
weeks later, while Mrs Strang was away, Miss Scott returned briefly
to pack her clothes, and had lunch with us. It quite frightened
me - we were all so pleasant and polite to each other - I don't know
what alternative there was, but we had been on such good terms
together earlier, and now one had the feeling that this could happen
to any of us and that our relationships were really very super-
ficial. Miss Crandle, half-heartedly but highly efficiently, had
become Acting Deputy in the meantime.
   I have described Miss Scott's downfall as an illustration, worse
than some, of the way we lose a steady trickle of staff (many not
mentioned in these pages). My farm assistant left soon afterwards,
partly it seemed because she had originally been selected by Miss
Scott. 'I'd never have appointed Miss Groves if I'd seen her hands
first,' said Mrs Strang, 'did you ever notice them?' (rather ugly
finger and thumb nails). I said I am little influenced by that sort
of thing (if I were, I might be tempted to see criminal-type ear-

lobes on Mrs Strang). Although it is a boon to me to have a full-time farm assistant, this proves awkward in practice since it plays into Mrs Strang's tendency to dislike, changeably, one of two partners in the same department. I felt vaguely guilty in not having guarded Miss Groves sufficiently, and determined to look after my assistant better in future. She was replaced almost immediately by Sarah Smythe, a delicate but courageous little girl recommended by a friend of mine. The question of a new Deputy also arose; Miss Crandle refused to take on the thankless task; Mrs Strang said I could not fill the post through being tied to the farm (thank God) so Miss Palethorpe offered herself after a week's deep reflection. She was not very popular, though regarded as reliable. On being asked my opinion I remember saying, 'Well, at least she's the devil we know.' We should have been amazed if we could have foreseen the future.

There is a sense, however, in which Mrs Strang could be said to possess psychic powers. She confided shyly to me at this point that, in addition to her strong chapel leanings, she is involved in spiritualism and visits a reputable medium. Apparently the medium had given ample warning of 'difficulty with a colleague' (a safe bet, surely) but that Mrs Strang would 'go straight on' while the colleague 'went off at a tangent'. Most of the staff have not known of this aspect of Mrs Strang, nor of her belief that she is occasionally possessed by a spirit other than her own.

Although we had been fairly solidly with Mrs Strang, somehow things changed after Miss Scott's departure. Enough dirty linen had been washed to leave a nasty taste in most mouths. In the effort of being at my most 'loyal', I was disillusioned, after a ridiculously long time. I began, after months of previous thought, to find a different attitude. I took things like truth, sincerity and loyalty for granted before coming here, but have needed to think a great deal since, and do not feel comfortable with any of them. I have never heard anyone talk of loyalty to themselves as our present Head does, nor expect it to be so blind. There is always the misery here of being torn between one's friends and doing what is expected of one for the big cause. In a small way it must be like relationships in Nazi Germany. Unless one is completely detached it is almost impossible not to zig-zag and finish shame-faced. Mrs Strang speaks often of our maintaining 'one standard', the highest standard, in short her own. But her standards are both too high (in practical ways) and too low for me. If I were ever to establish a more consistent relationship with her, I decided it would have to be the LCM or HCF of whatever there was - more a business relation and less personal, though none of us can avoid being personal really, living and working cheek by jowl. I was tired of going in and out of the 'dog-house', often not knowing why, so decided (after scores more incidents than described above) to detach myself a little from her standards and cleave to the remnants of my own.

We finished the winter off, short-staffed. Often I had almost the whole school on the farm, and would come into the warm house in the evening, sometimes to find that Mrs Strang and Miss Palethorpe had done my crossword puzzle in my absence. It is a daily pleasure to me, but she sees it as a job to be done. She was often hard on the farm-girls and, if anything went wrong, would threaten them with

selling up the farm. (Miss Groves took this seriously the first
time, and cried on the farm afterwards.) I did not discuss these
threats directly with the girls, who were invariably upset, but
continued discussing long-term policy with them: 'When Holly calves
next year', etc. Nowadays she rarely has me present when blasting
the farm-girls. But once, when Josie was on home-leave, she told
them Josie was a menace, then turned on Dot: 'But you wouldn't
agree - you're friendly with her!' Dot was frightened: 'Oh no, I'm
not, Mrs Strang, I'm not.' 'Don't give me that, you just let her
spoil your chances here, you are friendly with her.' Dot protested
almost hysterically and I, silent, badly wanted to say there is no
harm in being friendly.

My chief antidote for over a year now was attention to wild oats.
Daniel was developing his own farm adjoining his parents' land,
about twenty-six miles away, and we met through their employing one
of our girls. As they interviewed the girl partly here, Mrs Strang
knew them too from the start. In fact she occasionally said that
Mr Dawson had telephoned, with my thinking it was father not son.
But by New Year 19X7, Daniel managed to telephone me directly, and
we went out together for the first time. From the beginning it was
obvious that Mrs Strang visualized us at the altar, as it seemed a
perfect match on paper, and though it was enjoyable for a long time,
I felt pressurized to decide from the start, not least because
Daniel himself wanted a quick decision. Gradually I realized he
simply wished to marry and set up his own home - any wife would have
done. (If this appears that I'm not keen to marry, I am, but
perhaps my personality is more interesting than my appearance;
therefore limited choice is available and I'd rather stay single
than be tied evermore to a man who is dull during the day.)

Anyway, Daniel first called for me one evening, arriving early so
that I'd not quite finished a hasty bath. Mrs Strang, whether or
not with evil intent, had unexpectedly changed the timing of the
mid-week knicker change, when girls parade in the entrance hall
holding their knicker gussets out for Mrs Strang to observe, comment
upon (?) and sort for the laundry. Alice Sykes did her best to
shield him until I emerged but he must have thought it an odd
pantomime, being hustled a back way to asylum in the kitchen. Mrs
Strang tended to interfere, wanting to know where she stood perhaps,
though appearing keen to further my best interests - and under
instructions from the committee, she told me a year later, that she
was on no account to impede my marriage. I just wished they would
all mind their own business. According to Daniel, who was amused
but perplexed, she had at least two little cosy chats with him, not
unlike the over-frank talks she has with prospective husbands of our
old girls. Once was when she accompanied us to the Mayor's Ball in
Glebe, and he looked after her there and drove her home by pre-
arrangement after the first hour.

In these conversations she suggested to him that I am not
pleasant to live with (in the school) unless I have 'a man in tow',
'so do take her out frequently for all our sakes'. Whether this was
intended to encourage or discourage him was unclear. At an early
stage she asked me to drive her somewhere, giving her a typical
opportunity to tackle me towards the end of the journey when there
is just time for her to make her point without argument. 'Are you

seeing David tonight?' 'David who?' 'I mean Mr Dawes....' 'If you
mean Daniel Dawson, I am.' 'What are you going to do about him?'
'In what way?' 'Telling the wretched man where he stands....'
'I've made it clear from the start that I must have time. I'll try
to give you six months notice if and when the time comes.' 'Oh, I
understand - if he gets hurt, it won't be your fault.' No answer.
And another time, when I crept in at about midnight, it was to find
Mrs Strang awaiting me with an embarrassed Misses Palethorpe and
Crandle in attendance: 'Please in future refrain from carrying on
your courtship in the back drive - you've upset Evans' (evidently
Bill had reported an unknown car lurking). I replied with all
possible dignity, 'I shall certainly do no more courting on the
premises', and began to walk off. They all burst into peals of
laughter, having planned this as a joke. I forced a smile, saying,
'I daresay it is funny, but not very funny to me.'

Returning briefly to knicker-gussets, we have some routine
practices at Downcroft which must seem incredible to new girls and
outsiders. For example, no girl may leave a scrap of food on her
plate without first gaining permission from the member of staff on
duty. So one sits alone in state, with a little procession of
inedible bits of fat and gristle passing under one's eyes. If a
girl refuses food, she goes without food for the rest of that day.
When stricter members are on dining-room duty, a girl who is
unpunctual may have to eat standing up, or I believe Mrs Strang has
occasionally made a girl with 'disgusting table manners' eat from a
plate on the floor, like a dog.

We take ourselves so seriously that I sometimes find myself doing
something proverbial unawares. For instance, one of our geese flew
off once and the Head sent Mrs Briggs, Alice and me to look for it
in the van within a ten mile radius - we enjoyed the ride, without
realizing we were on a wild goose chase. Also I have told girls
there is no need to cry after a cow has kicked their bucket of milk
over; I have counted chicks before they were hatched, and once, when
my girls and I sat on the haystack in sunshine sewing sackcloth
aprons, we literally found ourselves searching for a lost needle.

CHAPTER 10

The girls' attitude to us was no longer very natural, nor often is ours to them. They are not allowed to mention their 'pasts', nor to ask 'personal questions' of the staff, so they constantly ask whether they can ask something before they proceed - for instance, 'Will you tell us again about your home?' Once I said my mother sent her love to them, and wanted me to say how well they had done in their external farm exams (they do surprisingly well, annually, irrespective of IQ apparently). I heard a girl whisper, 'Someone cares - makes you cry, don't it.' They were not supposed to make any remarks if I had to kill anything. In fact I dislike doing it, and manage better without remarks, but must offend the girls sometimes by seeming too matter-of-fact. Brenda, new and very talkative, said as I killed a duck, 'Don't you mind a teeny weeny bit, way down deep inside?' I replied primly, 'My way down deep inside is nothing to do with you, Brenda.' 'I'm ever so sorry, Miss Sparrow, I didn't mean....' Fortunately we all saw the absurdity of this, and Brenda used to tease me about it much later. The girls can be very tactful and considerate: 'Excuse me, Miss Sparrow, but you don't seem very happy today,' said Beryl. 'I am, thank you, just busy.' 'Well, if you don't mind me saying so, I think it would be better if you was to show you're happy a bit more!' She gave me an encouraging nod later.

One morning Mr Marsh commented to me that Mrs Strang has 'no eye for beauty', and I think he told her the same thing, as from us both, during a strong disagreement in the afternoon. She does knock things up very quickly and cleverly (gates, tables, etc., and a garage for my car which she mis-measured so that there is virtually no room for me to squeeze in alongside the garaged car) but they look knocked up and are not easy on the eye. At this point, the dividing door between farm and garden departments was locked by order, but Mr Marsh and I both have a key, and go through for an occasional chat. He resented a little the way I appeared to prosper on the farm, feeling I was undermining him, and I think she said things to both of us to make us distrustful of each other. After being told the above home-truth, Mrs Strang sometimes pointed out 'things of beauty' to me while I was driving her in the van. Once, going through a forest which I love, she said, 'Nice, isn't it!' I

just went 'Mmmm', and realized after a moment that she was only
referring to some litter.

It is not safe to let her think one has favourite girls (though
I try not to have favourites – the only apparent ones are those who
are more friendly to me) or to praise a girl's ability. Often she
seems intent on proving that one's faith is misplaced. New members
of staff, especially, sometimes cannot believe a particular girl is
naughty, but their eyes are rudely opened before long. One's most
reliable helper can be removed from the department – usually her
career choice – for a minor misdemeanor, and sometimes never allowed
to return. The 'staff girls' (one to wait on the Head and one upon
the staff) have a great deal to do and remember. They scuttle
around answering bells, running to and fro distractedly.
Occasionally in their haste, they fall upstairs carrying Mrs
Strang's tea-tray laid with her special china, and one finds the
girl crying amidst the confusion of broken, wet débris. 'Whatever
shall I do? How shall I tell her?'

This was another busy summer. It was still child's play to
manage the girls, and I had an exceptionally capable group on the
farm, where we enjoyed ourselves usually. But I remember Jean, then
an over-conscientious prefect, privately telling the group they must
support me, because I was so worried about the farm that I was
'reading and smoking in bed until four and five in the morning'.
Mrs Strang heard of this, and looked into it, in the presence of me
and my group. I kept trying to make clear that I sleep soundly as a
rule, but she would not listen, pretending it was none of her
business how I spent the night. Normally she is only too ready to
believe the worst (which I think harmful to the girls, when it is
held against them) but she irritates me when she pretends to be
disinterested in something which is unlikely to be true anyway.

One good thing was that Pearl eventually became a farm-girl for a
few months. Our former relationship remained dead but she was at
least ordinarily friendly in an extremely reserved way, and
apparently not unhappy on the farm. Later she was placed in a
domestic job about twelve miles away, but absconded before a bank
holiday weekend, and we did not see her again. Mrs Strang said we
could not involve the police during a bank holiday, and that she
quite hoped Pearl would become pregnant so she would no longer be
our responsibility. I went to collect her clothes from the
employer, and had a vague feeling that Pearl was hiding not far off.
We should have searched for her. I never met her mother, but Mrs
Briggs used to take Pearl once yearly to see her mother in the
subnormality hospital near London and said she was a nice person.

It must have been sometime that summer of 19X7 that Barbara
absconded. We had very few abscondings then and it was not something to undertake lightly. She went with another girl, did not get
far, and was sent up to her dormitory well after lights-out. The
current Head Girl, more 'useful' than some of the staff, called
Barbara a rat. Barbara reminded her that she herself had run away
the previous summer, and this piece of insolence was reported
immediately to the Head. Barbara was removed from bed, stripped,
and made to scrub the front stairs and corridor. This is hard to
believe, but she was completely nude, scrubbing on her knees, late
at night. The Head and staff sat in our sitting-room with the door

open, some colleagues showing signs of amusement - perhaps with
shock. I withdrew behind my newspaper, and regret having shown no
stronger signs of disapproval. So many surprising events happen
here that one tends to take outrageous treatment calmly. It shocks
one to imagine it in a different context, and I think only an
abnormal person could treat someone in this way.

In mid-summer my mother was seriously ill, and it was arranged
that I should take leave later (three weeks as it turned out) to
nurse her during convalescence. Sarah Smythe was eager to cope
alone and we got ahead with the work before I went. I returned to
find that Mrs Strang had 'worked wonders' on the farm in my
absence - she seemed nervous about my reaction - the number of new
gates and fences was bewildering but I managed to respond partially
to her need for praise. I saw later that she had fenced in one
field with no entrance at all for the tractor, that other gates were
too narrow, and she had put supports on much of the fencing which
stuck out like sore thumbs, decreasing the small amount of land
available. She may have thought I'd neglected the fencing but does
not realize that fencing is not a summer job at all. Mr Forbes, the
only farmer on the committee, snorted when he saw this uncon-
ventional fencing and said, 'You knock those bloody supports down
with the plough.' Easier said than done. On my second day back, I
unwittingly told Cissie to replace some equipment where it was
usually kept, but later, when I was alone on tea-duty, Mrs Strang
stormed in to ask who had put this equipment in the wrong place.
Cissie raised her hand and was verbally squashed; I (in front of all
the girls) explained that I had told her to. Mrs S shouted that
Cissie knew it now belonged elsewhere on the farm: 'You should have
told Miss Sparrow!'

Again soon afterwards, Mrs S found that the pump, for removing
surplus water from farm drains, was not being used regularly. She
now used pumping as a punishment and her rota was out of date,
though there is less need for it in summer. She spoke to me about
it, saying she would collect the farm-girls and punish them. I told
her quite politely that the pump is really my responsibility; that
the girls could hardly be expected to remember when I had forgotten.
A few moments later, when I was on cloak-room duty, she tapped me on
the shoulder and requested my presence in her office. The main
fault she had found in me to my face so far was my indecisiveness
- this time she said my aggressiveness was becoming unbearable.
Normally I am struck dumb on these occasions, but it struck me as so
funny that she should call me aggressive that I laughed and said,
'If you call that aggressive, you ain't seen nothink yet!' This
seemed to take her aback, and she dismissed me with a playful smack
after speaking more reasonably for a few moments.

Altogether things were unpleasant. Also three indoor colleagues
were smouldering about the changes brought about by Miss
Palethorpe's quick rise to power, and the fact that they had been
left to cope indoors while Miss Palethorpe stood watching all Mrs
Strang's recent outdoor labours. On the Sunday after my return I
was sick three times in the cloak-room without feeling exactly ill.
Sarah Smythe also started feeling sick, either through sympathy or
feeling I might desert her again (it was assumed that we had 'caught
a germ from the animals'). In the evening, while I was resting on

my bed, Mrs Strang came to see 'what was wrong', and questioned me
closely about the staff atmosphere. I agreed there was one, but had
nothing to say about it, as it was not my quarrel anyway. She
persisted, and I lay looking out of the window. She asked if it was
about Miss Palethorpe? 'Silence,' she said at one point, 'that
means "yes".' But it was too late for me to be caught like that.
She began to tell me how useful Miss Palethorpe is. I said I had
not yet complained of her laziness. She replied, 'No, you haven't',
and had to give up.

One of Mrs Strang's most nerve-racking methods is her habit of
interrogation. It is a far more lengthy, frequent and less subtle
process with the girls, but she tends to use it with colleagues when
they are already distressed, tired or off-colour, so that they are
more affected by it than they would be otherwise. She has not tried
it much with me, as I refuse to take part, though it seems childish
to say nothing. She does it brilliantly by raising the tension
until the questioned person is desperate, and then she is suddenly
kind, and the person breaks down completely, feeling only guilt and
gratitude for her kindness at the moment it was least expected. I
know this works like magic because I did it once myself uninten-
tionally with Babs, usually most reliable, when she was obstinate in
dallying over an urgent task. My anger grew in proportion to her
awkwardness until she was unreachable, fatalistically ready to be
hung for a sheep as for the initial lamb. I suddenly saw the misery
behind Babs's defiance, and spoke gently; she broke down and changed
completely, saying she was worried about her mother, and had had
tooth-ache for several days. But my unwitting manipulation of Babs
was probably all right, as we parted on good terms (with no question
in her mind as to whether I would report her, which is what they
most fear) and I did not try to hold her to ransom afterwards. Mrs
Strang somehow works on the person after they have cracked, trying
to bring them to a changed frame of mind for later use.

After Miss Palethorpe became Deputy our pattern changed. She and
the Head soon became inseparable as well as thinking alike. I will
not enlarge except to say that we (the lower staff) were affected
indirectly in that from now on we lived in two camps - Upstairs
(Head, Deputy, plus Miss Crandle often as a convenient trio) and the
rest of us Downstairs. The only problem about being downstairs is
that we rarely know what is planned aloft. The girls often go to
bed early, even straight after tea, when we are short-staffed, but
one tends not to know the time in advance. So if one is off duty
for the evening session, instead of having a two-hour class, but on
dormitory-duty later, one can be hanging about all evening waiting
to see when bed-time will come. Little Sarah Smythe had an eternal
cry in the staff room: 'What's happening - I say, do you know what's
happening?' In a short staff meeting about now, Mrs Strang reminded
us that our expected annual leave of eight weeks is actually 'six
weeks or eight if possible'; simultaneously she warned us about our
'manners' and left us to draw conclusions. Even so, she is good on
the whole about time off.

By now the staff were often changeable towards each other, though
it is remarkable how united we remain, and there is a special bond
between those of us who date from the former Head or even the pre-
Gracey days. Individuals of us were regularly invited fairly

formally to take tea upstairs (I went once); apparently Mr French
had advised Mrs Strang not to be so 'friendly' with her staff but to
maintain a wise distance. In spite of the 'divide and rule'
flavour, we continue friendly between ourselves even when one of our
number reports suspected misdemeanours. Dear Mrs Briggs, of whom I
am very fond, is most tempted (though we all are) to report her
colleagues, particularly my farm assistants, as she is quick to
pounce on the under-dog, yet often distorts her suspicions, and is
used as a kind of stool-pigeon. She has a tremendous need to
respect the Head and, though she has given many years of devoted
service here, I think she is now bewildered by the complexities of
the situation and worried about her own security.

Basically Mrs Strang is safer with us than she realizes, and does
not need to take quite such extreme precautions. For instance, when
it was reported to her that I occasionally lit a cigarette from the
one-bar electric fire in the staff-room, she could easily have asked
me not to do so, but instead she wired a thick metal painted grid
onto the fire, which smells strongly when heated, and simply acts as
a challenge to me for further malpractice. On one occasion Miss
Dale (the person who originally handed over the farm to me) visited
for lunch with the first head of Downcroft. I was greatly looking
forward to showing Miss Dale the farm, and Harmony after her
accident, and the new cows and sows bred from stock she had known,
but Mrs Strang said she herself would show them the farm. I argued
politely at some length but she insisted that I must rest in my
lunch-hour. I whispered to Miss Dale, 'It doesn't look as if I can
come, does it?' 'No, not unless you knock the bloody woman on the
head.' Apparently they shed tears on driving away from their visit
to Downcroft, where they both worked earlier for several years. Mrs
Strang would have made a better impression on them had she not
feared treason. At Christmas particularly, I hear from many people
I am tacitly expected not to hear from, as we are supposed not to
keep in touch with former colleagues who have left under a cloud.
Several members of staff, independently, wonder about the safety and
privacy of their in-coming letters and out-going telephone
conversations. Even though I make elaborate arrangements to avoid
detection, I tend to be asked directly whether I am corresponding
with so-and-so.

The prefect system operates directly from upstairs. It has
always seemed an almost evil thing - a source of strength to the
Head and a stumbling-block to the rest of us. Perhaps we come here
(staff and girls) comparatively innocent, and learn fast to be self-
righteous, to betray and blackmail, to spy and report, to retain our
individual reputations by destroying those of others, and to sink or
swim in this atmosphere. Even if the prefect system is on a small
scale and cleverly intangible, it is a very real thing. Even if it
has been so criticized by external officials that it is no longer
really acknowledged, it still goes on. The Head Girl and individual
prefects tend to show a certain pattern. Outwardly she washes a
lot, makes small, fussy movements, and adopts a whining voice (to
show she really has no choice) while bullying the herd. She is not
necessarily a 'natural leader' unless it seems best to link her
energies on the side of authority. If she is not as zealous as she
should be, she may be threatened with loss of home-leave or

discharge, which is her main goal. A girl has a quick rise to
power, and often has an equally quick fall, but is delighted again
when prefects are in such short supply that she is given a second or
third chance. She may be absolved from past sins, in order that the
girls will have 'nothing on her' and she is free to report them.
Reporting involves a lot of scuttling about, with lengthy
questioning and further disclosures, while the staff downstairs do
not quite know what is happening, and may themselves be discussed
privately with prefects. Rules are legion, and keep changing (which
in itself implies their unnecessary nature) and are delivered
straight to the girls, with the idea that they, however dim, know
the rules even if some of the staff do not. Most rules are phrased:
'No girl....' In general we suffer the prefect system in silence,
with little influence and an occasional protest. 'I'm a prefect,
Miss Sparrow! I never thought I'd be - I'm really going to try
now - my mum won't half be pleased!' 'Oh yes,' I say weakly. Very
occasionally I give a new prefect a little pep-talk about her
function being mainly to help other girls, and ask her to remember
how it felt before she was a prefect, but mostly this is useless and
merely causes extra conflict in the new prefect.

One night in late summer, Alice Sykes was very angry. It had
come back to her through a kitchen-girl that a prefect had said Mrs
Strang had said she (Alice) was no longer on duty at meal-times
because her discipline was poor. Alice was a great believer in 'not
bottling things up'. She released her anger loudly to me and my
assistant. She was quite funny when angry, and quick to see this
herself. Soon we had laughed the worst over. I advised her to
think twice before tackling Mrs Strang, and to wait anyway until she
had cooled down, as she was no match. Next day, a prefect reported
that Miss Sykes was heard to have whispered to another colleague in
her first wrath: 'I'm damn well fed up with the whole damn shoot!'
After much interviewing, Alice, off duty in bed, was faced by Mrs
Strang and a prefect, and asked if she had said this phrase. Driven
too far, she said yes she had, and would say it again and
immediately did. Next Mrs Strang enquired of me how much I had
known, and said 'the straight thing to do' would have been to take
Miss Sykes to her the previous evening. 'I've been put in a very
awkward position, because you know I always take your part on
principle.'

Alice gave in her notice. She had been seriously out of favour
for many months, receiving numerous duplicated notes - a bad
sign - about her kitchen work. She wanted me to leave too,
encouraging me by saying constantly, 'When a door closes, a window
opens', but I would not consider it unless it were to be married.
Whilst serving notice, Alice really only had me in whom to confide,
which could be nerve-racking with her carrying whisper. I think
most of us have the feeling (not expressed) that Mrs Strang is like
some dragon in a fairy tale which preys on a community and is
placated by being given a 'maiden' at regular intervals (i.e.
Dorcas, Miss Scott, Alice and several lesser victims). We used to
wonder, even laughing about it, 'Who's going to be next?' While the
group was somehow each time grateful to the maiden for focusing
attention on herself, it was necessary - if we were to appear 'loyal
to the one standard' - to shun her, which means that leaving is a

lonely process. I stood by Alice, to some extent, because she had
to have someone; also I must have had some strange idea that, if I
shared in this with Alice, it might not happen directly to me in
future.   She found it difficult to get another job and was short of
money. Her testimonial from Mrs Strang was not enthusiastic,
especially between the lines, so I perhaps wrongly wrote her one
myself (and for subsequent leavers) saying that I'd worked with her
for over two years.   I do not see why unwilling leavers should be
further penalized after departing from Downcroft.   I was away when
Alice actually went (though I continue to see her) and I was told
she hopped breathlessly into a taxi, having worked until the last
moment to leave her kitchen department in good order.   The girls
were taken for a long walk so that they should not see her
departure.   Her name was not officially mentioned again, except that
there was said to be a bad smell in her room and kitchen.   It is
degrading to leave only a smell as one's legacy here - currently I
am trying to get everything on the farm into near-perfect order
during my last eight months, but rather doubt whether this will make
any difference.   The girls loved Alice, and she could have been
excellent with them in other circumstances - a very homely, warm-
hearted woman, and a good cook. They were unable to speak of her
once she left, except occasionally to me. It must be confusing for
them, unless slightly comforting that we are in the same boat, when
members of staff leave in semi-disgrace.

    Shortly before Alice left, Harmony was very ill again. We found
her collapsed one morning. I was closely attached to Harmony, with
faith in her ability to survive against great odds. The vet thought
she would die that night. I stayed with her, while she showed no
intention of dying, and I spent my spare time in her loose-box for
two days. Meanwhile Mrs Strang wanted her either to live or die
quickly. Eventually I said that if Harmony were my cow I would
continue indefinitely, but in this case the committee had better
decide at their meeting two days hence. I was called into the
meeting and told they felt Harmony must 'go to market', but they
hoped I would not be upset. (When this phrase is used, it somehow
makes me feel I ought to be much less upset than I would be
otherwise.) I agreed, saying it would be best for her to be shot on
the premises rather than transported to an abattoir. I arranged
this for the following morning (a Saturday) and felt awkward about
continuing to look after Harmony during her last night - like the
conflict prison officers have over someone due to be hanged. I was
secretly depressed when Harmony took a real turn for the better in
the middle of the night, with her temperature almost up to normal,
because I doubted whether Mrs Strang would allow the decision to be
reversed. So it was something of a relief to find first thing on
Saturday morning that Harmony had dislocated a hind leg, presumably
in struggling to rise to her feet, and her death was now essential.
At 10.30 a.m., when the slaughterer's lorry was due, the whole
school was kept indoors, and I returned to tell them when it was
over. It happened very quickly, almost while I was removing her
halter, and I remember Harmony's momentary look of surprise.

    Later that Saturday morning, two non-farm girls absconded and
were brought back just after lunch. Mrs Strang dealt with
Christine, and turned to a more defiant Doreen, telling her to

remove all her clothes in the entrance hall. Doreen was
truculent - Miss Palethorpe, Alice and I joined in to help. She
refused to take her knickers off because she was menstruating (only
Mrs Strang knew she would be allowed to retain her long vest). It
is difficult to believe that we removed her pants forcibly. I can
only think I helped because (a) one must always appear to be on the
staff side; (b) I have to force myself to join in these scenes at
all but became expert in Gracey days, and find it best to join in
quickly without thinking of more important alternatives as an
excuse; (c) I was dazed about Harmony. I think Alice and I were not
much help, and only held Doreen's arms. At one point it looked as
though we were fighting a losing battle, so Mrs S and Miss
Palethorpe began to laugh, implying they were still in control, weak
only through amusement. It was most degrading to us all. Later
that afternoon, I took Christine over some fields outside the
premises to retrieve the two girls' school uniform dumped in a
bramble patch. When I finally managed to snatch a few minutes'
privacy in my room in the evening, it was too late to be able to
shed a tear about Harmony. This is what often happens - I must have
a lot of tears stored up somewhere.
     As regards violence, it is clearly best to by-pass it whenever
possible. We well know the early signs, and there are ways of
decreasing them without losing authority. But if a girl becomes
really violent, there is often no choice but to tackle her
physically. But this can still be done reasonably gently, and I
virtually never felt we were tougher than we had to be in the Gracey
era. Once it starts, anybody (girl or staff) is likely to get the
odd bruise, scratch or bite, but one does not 'take it personally'
because the girl is beyond taking normal responsibility for her
actions by that stage, although I have known individuals be
resistant with some limbs more than others, according to which of us
were holding these. But Mrs Strang tends sometimes (a) to control a
violent girl at arm's length by the back of her hair; (b) to lose
self-control if she is at all hurt, and attack the girl (and
sometimes it seems as though she almost pretends to be hurt in order
to justify attack); (c) if she is slightly hurt, her injuries
recover slowly, and she keeps reminding the girl of it, though the
girl will feel very guilty once she is over her temper tantrum. On
the other hand, Mrs Strang occasionally almost ignores a violent
girl if she does not feel we are strong enough to win, and this
again is disconcerting when the situation really demands some firm
control.
     I have always had this conflict about supporting the Head. The
Head of a place like Downcroft is obviously under great strain,
perhaps mainly because her own ability to keep discipline is of
supreme importance, and nobody on the spot is in a stronger position
than she. Unhappily, this strain appears to play into Mrs Strang's
weakness of being unable to appreciate good and bad elements in the
same person simultaneously. It is a fact of life that everybody is
a mixture (and I puzzle frequently over Mrs S's peculiar mixture,
and then feel guilty to be trying to judge whether she is 'mad or
bad') and I think we could be more relaxed if we recognized this
openly. Although I am reasonably confident over my own behaviour in
ordinary circumstances, I have found it confusing to be treated in

rapid succession as though I were either entirely good or bad, never
both at once. It must be far more confusing to the girls, who are
less sure of themselves. There is a separate strain in that the
girls often seem keen to discover whether we are good. They tend to
feel 'put away' as punishment when they come here, and their
assumption must be that, if they are bad, their trainers will be
good. They half want the assurance of knowing that we are good and
can accept them, and half want to prove we are no better than they
are. It would be much easier to help them cultivate their own
goodness if we could all relax a little. Another factor is that the
girls show a great need to see the Head as a specially good person,
as a kind of ideal mother on a grand scale, so it confuses them if
her behaviour seems an odd mixture, and they become increasingly
convinced of their own badness. It works both ways, and hurts
everybody concerned.

Sometimes a girl, in a confiding moment, asks me my opinion of
her - they are surprisingly keen to know, and hold on to it afterwards. For instance, Kathy asked me when I was too exasperated with
her to say more than, 'You're a mixed blessing', and she reminded me
ever after 'I am a mixed blessing, Miss Sparrow, you did say so
yourself!' Of course I am often impatient and cross with them,
though they are anxious to be on easy terms again and I am always
touched by their formal little phrase 'Will you accept my apology?',
whereas the higher staff reply that they are interested in improved
deeds, not in glib words of repentance. I used to dislike showing
my ignorance of plans, etc. in front of the girls, but the fact is
obvious now. We are quick in picking up information without
exposing ourselves. These girls are probably quicker in sensing
atmospheres than ordinary schoolgirls. They are well aware when any
of the staff are 'in trouble'. I conceal the fact as far as
possible when I am, and they would not dare mention it directly to
me, but often they are extremely kind. As some colleagues tend to
turn to the girls for sympathy, this is another complexity. I have
heard a girl say to Tommy, upon her receiving a summons, 'Oh, Miss
Thomas, I do hope you're not in trouble!' 'So do I,' replied Miss
T, with less surface calm than many girls would achieve.

It needs quick thinking before one decides to report a girl for
serious or trivial misbehaviour; on the whole it seems preferable to
be involved if one wishes to see a minimum of justice done, rather
than have a prefect report distortedly. Even so, the outcome is
highly unpredictable: sometimes, if one is out of favour, the girl
may be considered extra correct; if one is in favour, she may be
regarded as extra bad, or if one is out of favour, she may be
heavily punished just to compensate for one's own softness. It is
not surprising that Mrs Strang considers me indecisive when so much
has to be weighed up - she must hate the way I seem to have a poor
opinion of her, in comparison with others. But when girls are
continually punished for something they have not done, and have
missed the preliminary fun of doing it, they naturally in the end
'stop trying' and take what fun they can get. It disillusions them
completely - one of the worst things here is to see adolescents,
still children at heart, become embittered, not expecting a fair
deal, let alone kindness, from authority. It has a bad effect on
people's characters when the worst is automatically believed, and
acted upon.

In trying to present a concise case when reporting (i.e. when trying to speak before a prefect puts a spoke in the wheel) I am usually interrupted: 'Send for her!' 'May I just finish...?' 'You've told me enough - all of a piece, already had complaints... thoroughly nasty piece of work....' It is impossible to argue in the girl's presence once she is summoned; often she is accused through you of doing something she has not done or, if two girls are involved, one of them may take all the blame. Once, after months of hearing Della's morbid talk on the farm, I asked her to give it a rest. She replied that I must try to understand she is mad. I, losing patience, said, 'You know ruddy well you're not mad.' As a prefect had overheard me swear, I decided to make my own explanation, but it was Della who came off worst, threatened with dire consequences if she did not immediately cease her attention-seeking behaviour, and she slunk off with a reproachful glance.

The girls are amazingly philosophical about all the above, on the surface. At first I expected them to rebel, but it is really too hard to kick against the pricks. Many of them have been fighters for years through necessity - I think they would break out if they received anything approaching fair treatment, but they seem to recognize the ruthlessness. We are not even on the level of justice which demands an eye for an eye - in return for a tooth, one might lose both eyes and all teeth. But the girls are very resilient - it needs constant nagging and what Mrs Strang calls 'vigilance' to keep them up to standard. She has an uncanny knack of jumping heavily (on girls or staff) just when the person is so crushed already that they have a little desperate courage stored up. Unrest is dispersed by further reprisals. Little consideration is shown to a girl who is being difficult because she is worried, perhaps about her home.

Of course I have seen here what happens when things get out of hand, and would not care for a repeat performance, though I was happier in those days on the whole. I am recognized by the girls as a firm member of staff and they quite appreciate ordinary firmness for safety. They toe the line to some extent for expediency, but also tend to compare themselves with adult prisoners, perhaps because that is more glamorous than being a naughty girl, and also it is a subtle reproach to the staff. Dostoevsky has an appropriate paragraph: 'Some people think that, if convicts are well fed and well kept and all the requirements of the law are satisfied, that is all that is necessary. This is an error, too. Everyone, whoever he may be and however downtrodden he may be, demands - though perhaps instinctively, perhaps unconsciously - respect for his dignity as a human being.... And as he really is a human being, he ought to be treated humanely. My God, yes! Humane treatment may humanize even one in whom the image of God has been long obscured' (which of course it hasn't, in our girls). Respect for personality has, for the last five years, been in short supply at Downcroft. Miss Gracey somehow did not respect herself enough; Mrs Strang seems to respect only herself and not even, ultimately, that.

We thought for some time that Mrs Strang meant what she said, because she said so; she told us she had twenty-six years' experience of social work and knows people inside-out. I did not think her lack of paper qualifications mattered, although I see the truth of someone's remark that professionally trained people do

usually have certain values. Mrs Strang constantly makes enormous
threats which are impracticable - not to mention undesirable, and
not even expedient because it seems irresistible to our girls to
test the validity of a threat. There is no sense in threatening to
stop all letters in and out of the school for a whole month, unless
a missing beret (which may actually be lost) is produced immediately. I don't know how far our deteriorating behaviour is due to a
fairly general belief that delinquent girls are growing increasingly
difficult, because it is difficult to see what they are really like
under these conditions. I sometimes try to imagine what a
particular girl might have been like with Miss Gracey. Mrs Strang
seems to keep looking ahead to brighter days, once some unhelpful
element has been purged away. Inevitably I wonder frequently
whether she is really responsible for her own actions, and it does
seem surprisingly as though she is not, which means that advice and
warnings from outside are not effective. She clearly makes heroic
efforts to control herself and this shows mainly in the way she
keeps all the rest of us so organized, and all the environment so
taped, with these little barbed-wire paddocks, and everything so
unnaturally clean, even the drains. But she seems too afraid of bad
things happening to be able either to control herself or to relax.
Her own childhood sounds to have been strict, and I am sorry, but it
seems a pity to propagate it here.

If a bore is someone who says everything, my excuse is that this
is by no means all. (The original version of this diary, even
though it ran to over 150,000 words, did not include everything.)
One further incident in the late summer of 19X7 is worth mention.
When the exceptionally 'useful' Head Girl was demoted, there seemed
no one to take her place. I said to my colleagues as a joke, 'One
day we'll wake up and find Jenny is Head Girl', and to our surprise
this happened. She was a transfer who came here as a last resort to
try farming - big, nearly six feet tall, unusually intelligent, with
a reputation for taking advantage of weakness. The new Deputy Head
Girl was also a farm-girl, another bright, fairly deep person. I
was so much on the defensive, foreseeing trouble, that I jumped too
quickly. On her first day as Head Girl, Jenny reported another girl
who did better work than she, and I was annoyed, without saying so,
to lose this girl from the farm as a result. The following day,
while slower-witted members were engrossed in working for their
external farm exams, I found Jenny and her Deputy throwing eggs at
each other. Unwisely I told them that as they were so quick to
report others without consulting me, they could now report
themselves. I partially retracted this on hearing their excuse, but
said they were still to tell Mrs Strang. They told her all,
including my retraction. I was summoned post haste, found myself in
more trouble than they were, and thought they would all hear my
heart beating. When Jenny's turn came, she took off her Head Girl's
badge with a martyred air, while Mrs Strang shouted that she was not
to dare remove it until it was taken from her. The next day I told
Jenny I realized it was not easy being Head Girl, and that I did not
want to hamper her, and she was all right with me then.

Meanwhile I was seriously in Mrs Strang's bad books, and would
have remained so except for the problem of Pauline - a new girl,
rapidly becoming mentally unstable, whom I just managed to control

by using her native Cumberland accent sometimes. (We had already
had a scene with her when she absconded, and was caught near the
river by the headmistress, Head Girl and myself. She was wild, and
difficult to handle while kicking in leather boots. Both Heads
(girl and woman) began hitting her; I told the former to stop, while
the latter accidently hit my face on the upstroke when hitting
Pauline on the downstroke, and I saw red for a moment. Afterwards,
Mrs Strang asked for a written list of our damages - my list
consisted of a kick on the elbow from Pauline and a bang in the face
from herself.) Now, on top of the Jenny situation, Pauline seemed
to crack when Miss Palethorpe shouted at her early one morning. She
was put into detention, her chief cry (which I could hear in bed)
being, 'Just wait till Miss Sparrow comes on duty - she'll soon
settle the bloody lot of you!' But Pauline was only fit for a
mental hospital by this time. It took a day or two to arrange, and
meanwhile several of us had to hold her each time the doctor
visited. At one point the detention room door blew shut and we were
all locked in automatically until a girl rescued us. It felt very
odd, and I cannot think what it feels like to be locked up for very
long (longer than the permitted twenty-four hours, sometimes, by
various strategies such as starting a second twenty-four hours after
a brief bath) - especially being isolated, not knowing what is to
happen; and some girls are terrified out of their wits by being
locked up at all.

After Alice left, Mrs Briggs was in hospital for many weeks in a
very weak state though she returned and slowly recovered. Meanwhile
I spent hours in the staff-room (often waiting for dormitory-duty)
with just Tommy and Sarah Smythe. Sometimes we were almost beyond
talking to each other. Sarah, like Alice, enjoyed the work here in
some ways and wanted to stay, but found it unbearable, so Sarah left
too. She was protected to some extent here by frequent visits from
influential relatives - though Mrs Strang's jaw dropped on learning
too late quite how important one aunt and uncle were (magistrate and
MP, later a cabinet minister). She was quite rude to them on their
short visit, of which the highlight, so they said, was watching me
give a drench to Hat-trick who perversely jerked her head at the
crucial moment, drenching me instead with the purplish medicine. At
this time we were short-staffed and extra busy with recalls and with
girls in local lodgings, some of whom did not last long anywhere,
and deflated our low reputation in the neighbourhood. After Alice
went, we were without a cook for months - everything seemed a bit
colourless, even the food. I was lonely, within Downcroft itself,
during these months. During my last few years here I have developed
a very private habit of telling the pigs how I feel, just in a few
words, on my nightly round of the farm after dark. A pen of
baconers will rise to their feet at my approach and listen intently
with pricked ears and expressionless little eyes into which I can
read any amount of goodwill and sympathy.

I forgot to say that Jenny (ultimately in Broadmoor) soon failed
as Head Girl, went on hunger-strike, and then ran away in the rain,
wearing only underclothes and a cotton overall, without money.
After a few weeks she telephoned Mrs Strang from London (previously
unknown to her) saying she had found employment and a bed-sitter,
and asking permission to stay. Mrs Strang did not want her back, so

I was sent to the northern suburbs of London to see if Jenny's
circumstances were suitable. It was good to see her after climbing
three flights of stairs to her attic, though our meeting seemed like
a dream. She was very hospitable, made a cup of tea, and had bought
a packet of my customary cigarettes. She had picked up cheap
clothes and was pretending to be an agricultural student. I think I
appreciated how hard it is to adjust to life 'outside' when I saw
her spotless room, with a menu, time-table and list of rules pinned
on the wall. I took her out for a large meal, said good-bye, wrote
a report on the station, and she was allowed to stay (my conclusion
being that she was better off there than in Downcroft, even if I'd
observed an elaborate hoax).

In early autumn, Mrs de Villiers came to see round the farm. Mrs
Strang, and I, imagined she would be very pleased with everything.
The 'three year extension plan' had been completed in one year, in
so far as it was ever a practical proposition; by now I have
increased productivity nearly ten-fold, estimating to spend over
£2,000 and realize over £3,000 annually from a small acreage. But
Mrs de Villiers seemed dissatisfied. She complained of 'the lack of
music' on the farm, and she explained the 'therapeutic value' of
ducks quacking, pigs grunting, calves lowing, etc. to a delinquent.
This seemed far-fetched to me, but on looking up the word
therapeutic in the dictionary, I began to see that she missed the
old freedom, and indeed that therapy is lacking here. I still
visualize the farm in its earlier beauty even if it is festooned in
barbed wire now.

Several people have found it almost impossible to understand why
I have stayed so long here. It is my first job and I do not expect
to have the same feeling again of being absolutely in my element
while farming and teaching delinquent girls. Farming is an
excellent medium for reaching them, through the animals often, and
our joint work together is very pleasant indeed. (Though this year
of 19X7 I felt tearful on my birthday, which happened to be my day
off; that I was getting old at twenty-six, with an uncertain future.
I was near tears as colleagues came in and out of my room after
breakfast with good wishes, but Mrs Strang, at her best, shielded me
with my newspaper and told them I was finding the light trying.)
Other reasons for not leaving this terrible place until 19X9 are
that you have never finished on a farm - there is always another
calf coming to maturity or another crop to be harvested or sown.
Also it will be impossible to find another job enough like this; I
will be unable to keep in touch probably after leaving; to leave
under a cloud makes it hard to find another job, and I was
(foolishly) always hoping Mrs Strang would change and was not going
to be pushed if she didn't, and finally there comes a point when it
takes more strength to leave than it does to stay. But the main
attraction is feeling completely myself in our joint work on the
farm - some of the girls think I was born here!

CHAPTER 11

From now on, during my last two years here, the plot thickens
slightly, although there is also a sense in which it tails off. It
was a real landmark to me, and has continued important, when two new
members of staff came in September within a fortnight of each other
and, though different in themselves, I felt on the same wave-length
with both.

Joyce Romanes, soon known as Romany, came as my new farm
assistant (the most capable since Iris) - plump and jolly, appearing
refreshingly uncomplex, like students I had enjoyed formerly when
training, and I was relieved to feel she might be comparatively
unsettled by all the wheels within wheels at Downcroft. Anna
Herrison, also in her early twenties, arrived straight from a
postgraduate course (she and I being the only graduates here) to be
our new schoolteacher, replacing Miss Palethorpe who was now well
established as Deputy. I have even more in common with Anna - a
thoughtful, warm-hearted person, gentler in her stimulating ideas
than Dorcas, and more able to put her thinking into words than I am.

On the whole, things suddenly seemed more normal. Mrs Strang is
usually pleasant to new people, and I was happier now they had come.
Beforehand I had grown rather desperate, as there had seemed no one
on the staff with whom I could really talk, or who shared quite the
same basic values. Naturally new members of staff, particularly if
it is their first post in 'a maladjusted school', tend to accept
what they find. Anna soon noticed something I had been doing for
years vaguely unaware: that is, that I do not look at Mrs Strang
when I disagree with her remarks. It is an easy way of showing
disagreement - if you look at her, she seems to try to extort
approval. She rarely speaks of the girls without a sneer, as though
they are our natural enemies, and seems always on the defensive,
taking advance precautions against potential ill-wishers - though we
seem to wish her surprisingly well, considering.

If anything, staff relations are more complex here than ours with
the girls. Mrs Strang, when fonder of me, often pointed out how
alike she and I are, though I must say I fail to see it, except that
we both have an 'all or nothing' attitude. Mine may have developed
partly to offset hers, as it is simply not safe, I think, to
compromise with her, though it would be a great relief in one way to

78

do so. In trying to find a balance in the discomfort here, I seem
to have grown far more idealistic than I am by nature, and this
perversity probably has in turn an unfavourable effect on Mrs
Strang. It might seem ridiculous to compare the practice of brain-
washing with our Downcroft experience, which is a flea-bite in
comparison with the real thing - but the principle is the same,
although we are in no physical danger. At least in enemy hands you
do not have to try to co-operate and understand, and it is not
assumed that you are on the same side; the issues at stake may be
clearer, so I think the spiritual peril is comparable. It would be
easier without the daily strain of living in the shop-window of such
an emotionally explosive place, and if one did not care about all
the inmates. The above may be nonsense - all I know is that it is
possible to experience some degree of inner torment here - indoors
not outdoors.

I think most of the staff, past and present (more people than
appear in these pages) have been 'dedicated' enough not to dwell
overmuch on their own personal difficulties and humiliations. Yet
Mrs Strang is clever enough to by-pass the main issue of the girls'
welfare, and bring things to a head on a petty, personal level.
Female colleagues are commonly supposed to fight like cats, so
outsiders are not surprised when a steady stream of women apparently
lose their sense of proportion. Most of our staff at heart have not
been cats (too busy for one thing), and we are all faulty of course
in some ways but normally would have the overall strength to carry
our weaknesses. We all tend to become heated when personally
slighted in our work, partly because Mrs Strang is like a conjuror
in distracting one's focus from the dangerous issue of our treatment
of the girls on to something trivial. She has been described as
'diabolically clever' on this level, and can appear to be in the
right. Partly too, it is because we bottle up a series of pricks,
and then suddenly let fly when the last straw descends. Mrs Strang
sometimes returns from leave in belligerant mood, perhaps having
consulted her medium, eager to precipitate any embryonic antagonism
at the earliest possible moment, then able to tie up the person with
dexterity and push them on their way. I think several of us have
had as good brains as she, but she can run rings round us. I can
predict a little latterly because I know the pattern, but am
frequently amazed at her resourcefulness. It is extraordinary how
many birds she can kill with one well calculated stone.

There is also the conflict about warning new members of staff.
This time with Anna and Romany was the only time I did so to any
large extent. I think it was because, first, I did not want them to
become involved as I had, although I really might have saved my
breath, as people can learn only through their own experience. What
happened later would probably have happened anyway, and in the
process I somehow became involved myself all over again in spite of
having reached the best stance open to me, earlier. Second, I had
been worried for a long time, and with the relief of having a
sympathetic audience I talked far too much - in a manner which may
have overwhelmed them, though I was too far gone to take note. I
did almost decide at the beginning not to say anything until they
had had a chance to see for themselves, but in the event I blurted
confidences indiscriminately. Anna is better than I am at finding a

wise confidant from outside - with her coming, we had the benefit of
her former tutor, whose words I seized upon eagerly at second hand.
Until now, my own confidants were limited to the cows and pigs, who
of course never uttered a word in reply, and to my neighbouring
farm-worker Mr Laycock who gave practical help occasionally, and to
my garage man. My ancient car needed frequent repair and
eventually: 'You know I told you the engine was dropping out of the
chassis? Well, it's dropped!' On this occasion, I was telephoning
him whilst on the verge of a sneeze; he must have thought I was
crying, and I found it most comforting when he said, 'Don't worry,
Miss, I'll always help you.'
   We had never previously had so many cars here, and we were all
more mobile for a time, slipping out whenever there were at least
two of us off duty, to the special delight of Mrs Briggs. Later we
felt less free - Romany and I were told that one of us must always
stay around in case there was 'an emergency on the farm' - illogical
when I was often required for chauffering while without a farm
assistant. Another hindrance was a new idea that I should spend two
of my few free evenings 'on duty by Arrangement'. I never knew what
this meant, but used to amuse myself in the staff-room or do the
farm accounts, waiting for an Arrangement to be made. I have
several outside friends nearby or in neighbouring counties, but have
not found many people who understand enough of our peculiar
situation to make discussion worthwhile.
   That early autumn I put five girls into farm jobs, mostly long
distances away, and missed this excellent group on our own farm, as
there was a very mixed, unskilled bunch in their stead. We also
concreted the farm yard and drive, organized by Mrs Strang, who did
all the 'plodging' herself. Romany managed the concrete-mixer, the
girls carted gravel, sand and cement in wheel-barrows, while I
continued routine farm work and tried, not always successfully, to
steer girls and animals from A to B without their stepping on wet
concrete, and Miss Palethorpe stood watching our labours. Mrs
Strang was engrossed with this for days, making a good job of the
complex yard but a mess of the drive, having laid thin concrete on
surface mud in unsuitable weather instead of making clinkered
trenches. The net result was that I was no longer allowed to have
lorries coming up the farm drive in case her efforts cracked. She
rarely visits the farm in winter, but spends long summer days
outside, and had the mad idea of rolling soil onto my paths, which
then look smart in summer but are ankle-deep in winter mud, making
farm buildings more difficult to keep clean.
   The first major event in this period was at the end of September,
when we began to have much more absconding. Mrs Strang usually
creates some lever to quieten the girls while she is on leave, and
each one knows that an individual report will be made on her return,
leading to prolonged questionings and judgment. One Wednesday after
lunch I noticed numerous girls crying while I was on cloak-room
duty, and then found my farm group wailing in the boiler-house. I
thought they had been quarrelling, and asked them to put it aside
temporarily because I was expecting the ministry vet to come and
test the cows for TB. 'But you don't understand, Miss Sparrow, this
is going to be a closed school!' A closed school, described in
dreadful terms, had been threatened before if there was any more

absconding, but this time it made a deep impression and put the
lower staff in an awkward position. The girls questioned me all
afternoon: 'Will there be cows/pigs/farm, etc. if this is a closed
school?' I didn't answer directly until after the weekly service at
5 p.m. (when the chaplain spoke about Truthfulness!) In the evening
I replied that this is a farm school, and I felt sure would continue
to be so. I told Mrs Strang at supper-time that this was awkward,
but she said little in reply. Next day she went off for a short
holiday, and the girls knew that Miss Merton (inspector) would be
visiting the day after her return.

   While she was away, the girls became convinced that the threat
would be carried out - either someone did abscond or they thought
someone had or was trying to run away. One danger of threats is
that they may not work as anticipated. In fact the girls planned a
mass absconding, in order to leave before Downcroft became a closed
school (i.e. a stricter school, with more locks). Only eight
managed to get away, during the day and night before Mrs Strang's
return. They were picked up quickly by a number of us travelling
long distances both by train and van. Two made a damaging statement
to the police, saying amongst other things that Mrs Strang is a big
bully. Meanwhile she returned from holiday, very het-up, and I was
thankful to be away overnight fetching the last three girls back in
the van, with Mrs Briggs and Anna as escorts. These last three
would have been violent had we not been ordinarily friendly to them
on the journey back from London.

   Next day Miss Merton arrived. I felt sure Mrs Strang was in a
cleft stick, having brought on herself a mass absconding followed by
unrest, plus the girls' expectation of an immediate closed school
(which clearly could not happen), not to mention another allegation
to the police. I wondered what I would do in her shoes, and felt
all one could do would be to admit one's mistake to the committee
and inspectorate, and ask for support and advice. But Mrs Strang
kept up appearances somehow. Miss Merton must have smelt a rat but
did not locate it, I imagine. Afterwards Mrs Strang let the school
think she was generous enough only to punish the actual absconders,
who were moved in a body to one dormitory, where the windows were
screwed slightly open and a prefect slept across the locked door at
night. In this way the threat was executed without loss of face to
Head and Deputy. The lower staff were not able to discuss the
situation; for about a fortnight we found the girls extremely hard
to manage en masse. Mrs Strang partially withdrew, spending days in
bed, as is her normal practice when off duty. She pretended all was
well, so we continued by ourselves, feeling anything might happen,
and the extra tension very slowly eased.

   In October Anna had been advised by her former tutor that we
ought not to feel opposed to the Head without giving her a chance to
remedy the situation; we should say something openly, even if in a
very small way. In my eagerness to co-operate, I seemed to forget
that I had virtually been doing this very thing, certainly in a
small way, for two years already on my own muddled initiative.
However, Anna, Romany and I resolved to try to make a small
suggestion each at the next rare staff-meeting. I warned them
beforehand that I could not guarantee to play my part, as there is
little opportunity to speak, and (unbeknownst to the upstairs trio)

I hid my unloaded air-pistol under my chair beforehand to boost morale. (The air-pistol, permitted surprisingly by the Head, was purchased initially for crow-scaring, but I keep the pellets 200 miles away to avoid temptation.) I was so anxious to contribute that I asked politely quite soon whether the staff (downstairs) might share in the current marking system of the girls. Apparently I had anticipated the business of the meeting; a new scheme was outlined in which we take part still. I forget what Romany asked, but Anna said tactfully that she sometimes felt ignorant about plans. This surprised Mrs Strang, but she explained the difficulties and said she would inform us in future through a notebook in our sitting-room (which operates in fits and starts). Our suggestions seemed to have been accepted so reasonably that we felt elated, and that it was not so hard to approach the Head in a business-like way after all.

A few days later Mrs Strang explained to Anna that it was no use depending on me at all — that I was 'changeable and let people down'. I knew from Anna that this had been said, but tried to ignore it, not even being quite sure whether it was true, as I seemed to have become separated from a number of people already. The next morning Mrs Strang was so extra unpleasant towards me that I could not avoid appearing somewhat strained. After lunch I went to her sitting-room to explain about an epidemic of incurable fowl paralysis on the farm, because if the birds' temperatures were less than 110 degrees Fahrenheit the carcasses were fit for our consumption. After agreeing to take the risk of all this unfortunate roast chicken, she said, with face and voice like granite: 'What is the matter?' As it seemed childish to say nothing, I replied lightly, 'Oh, just a small thing that will come right in a few days.' She said, in a very overbearing way, 'That's no answer. I asked you what is the matter?' She must really have known. 'I prefer not to discuss it,' and I walked towards her door. 'Is it something personal?' I said yes, all quite quietly, and went downstairs again. A few moments later she called down that I'd gone out in a very rude manner while she was speaking to me, and she would not tolerate such behaviour. I said I was sorry but there was nothing else for it. (Anna tried for a long time to discuss things reasonably with Mrs Strang, and I think felt she should try to answer honestly any questions put to her. It comes more naturally to me to refuse to be drawn, and I had by now little guilt in maintaining silence when the Head tried to bluster me into useless discussion. Also I feel Mrs Strang intimidates and interrogates so many people that she deserves to be thwarted now and then.)

The next crisis, after the mass absconding, took place in mid-November. Mrs Strang was on holiday, and Miss Palethorpe (always more approachable when the Head is away) told me that Linda had broken down in her farm job in Muckshire, had retreated to her home, and refused to return because of her employer's swearing. I told Miss Palethorpe one expects some swearing on a farm but his must be excessive. She supposed 'damn' was all right, but I said there is a difference between being sworn with and sworn at (thinking of her own habit of shouting 'big, fat slob' at our girls) so we arranged to bring Linda back without her giving notice. Next morning I rose at 5 a.m., and collected Linda, silent, from her home, drove to the

back of beyond to fetch her belongings, heard the farmer's language,
and was glad to bring Linda back. We returned at 7.45 p.m., after
nearly 300 miles on a foggy day in an unheated van. I must have had
'flu without realizing, I thought I ached with mangel-pulling. On
return I bathed to get warm, then came down to the staff-room fire,
and to talk with Anna and Romany, before going to bed early. I did
rely on those evening conversations, and to be able to relax at the
end of the day with people who were safe to talk to, though it
sometimes meant waiting until certain members of staff had gone to
bed.

The following day I felt really ill, and knew by the end of the
morning's drag that it was 'flu, told the Deputy and went to bed.
The next day, Mrs Strang returned, rather distrait. She visited me
briefly and said a little ominously that I must rest as much as
possible while ill. There was a committee meeting the following
day, before which Mrs Strang tends to become heated. Beforehand,
when I remember my temperature was 102 degrees Fahrenheit (carcass
unfit to eat) she came to ask whether I'd known I had 'flu the day I
drove to Muckshire. I said I must have had it then, but had not
realized. She asked why I'd been mad enough not to go straight to
bed on return. I tried to explain. She was very angry, said we
were staying up much too late in any case, and in future the staff-
room was to be vacated by 10.30 p.m., a necessary rule if we were to
work properly. Normally I might have accepted this without arguing,
but felt at such a disadvantage that I sat up, and suggested this
was treating us like children; that we must have some freedom and
some time to call our own. She replied that, if we behaved like
children, we must be treated like children, and that we could meet
in our own rooms after 10.30. I said we would prefer to have the
choice of our own sitting-room. She lost her temper, saying I had
been the most polite member of staff and was now rude, and had been
the most willing member and was now unwilling to do anything extra.
I was too surprised to say anything. Finally, she said menacingly
that while I was ill I would have time to think things over, and had
better think very carefully indeed, and flounced out.

She returned a few moments later with Miss Palethorpe to adjust
my mattress, but really perhaps to see if I were unduly upset. I
just said thank you, as became the ex-most-polite person. Then I
went very hot and perspired through several nighties, and began to
feel better, physically. At 5 p.m. Anna and Romany came, and I told
them about it, most anxious that we shouldn't go to bed at 10.30.
They were angry, largely on my account, being treated like this when
ill, and said they would see Mrs Strang. Later in the evening, Mrs
Strang came again, this time softness itself; she rapidly turned my
room into a sick-room, and offered to wash me but I said I could
manage. She said I was silly to take any notice of what she'd said
earlier, surely I didn't think she had meant it? I replied non-
committally, having little idea what was happening. Then Anna and
Romany came again - Mrs S told them about our new bed-time but had
altered it to 11 p.m. A difficulty here is that one 'sides' with
someone and then regrets their co-operation. Apparently Romany had
been too hot-tempered, with mention of resignation. It is better to
manage alone really.

Mrs S came again that night, more self-possessed, and said she

would take my temperature herself, under my arm, 'because it is
possible to raise it by sucking it'. At 9 p.m. that same night she
sent for Anna, with Miss Palethorpe as witness, and questioned her
about everything she had thought since she came to Downcroft - for
three hours till midnight. Anna came briefly to tell me this the
following morning. She seemed wrung by the questioning, and the
unexpected kindness at the end, and said she must get right away as
it was her day off, Saturday. All she told me was that Mrs Strang
felt no need to talk with Romany, but would like to talk with me,
only I would have to take the initiative as she could not approach
me otherwise (after my elusiveness, I suppose). Next I was dazed to
find myself in Mrs Strang's bed, while my room was being cleaned;
she and Miss Palethorpe were solicitous and I was probably meant to
'talk' then, but didn't feel on safe enough ground. I said I would
like to talk with her in my room, if this were possible without an
emotional scene. She didn't seem keen but said she would spare a
short time in the afternoon. The GP came, asked me if 'everything
was all right', and said I could get up in a day or two when I felt
fit. Mrs Strang had kept a temperature chart since the previous
day, and it was going down now.

When Mrs Strang came to talk, I had my arm-chair ready for her at
a nice distance, and had only omitted to invite Miss Palethorpe as
witness. I felt very calm indeed for once, and almost (fool) in
control of the situation. I had planned a bit what to say, and
wanted to be convinced whether she felt satisfied with our treatment
of the girls. She was quiet and seemed reasonable. I felt it was
now or never, but we really got nowhere and she evaded anything of
importance. Whenever I started about the girls, she turned the
conversation back to me personally. She said I had 'changed' about
the time Alice Sykes left. I said it was long before that, which
surprised her. She said Miss Sykes hadn't been 'straight' with her,
and I said I didn't much mind whether Alice were straight or not, I
disliked the way she'd been treated. She mentioned Mrs Briggs
'making trouble' (i.e. reporting us to Mrs Strang) and I said this
really doesn't matter, we are fond enough of Mrs Briggs not to mind.
She said I might think she had 'interfered about Daniel', but it was
because the committee had told her she was on no account to
discourage me from getting married. I was touched by this, though
it didn't occur to me till afterwards that the committee may have
known nothing about it. I forget all we said, but towards the end I
tried to explain that I did want to be 'loyal', but could only be so
if I was able to say when I disagree, without having a scene. In
fact, I made an 'agreement' from my side while her side remained
undeclared.

Just then, Romany came in, after work, and apologized for
interrupting. But Mrs S snapped at her, 'She's all yours!' and left
hurriedly. She returned in the evening to take my temperature. I
said I thought there was no need to take it any longer, and I hoped
to get up next day or the day after. She said, particularly
malicious, that she would decide when we stopped taking it. She
removed the chart from my waste-paper basket, saying it would be
safer in her care. This really frightened me, as she knows that,
whereas some people tend to have a headache when they are inwardly
het-up, I tend to have a slightly raised temperature (investigated

earlier in hospital when I was a student) without feeling at all ill
with it. I knew her well enough by now to realize that she could
keep me in bed indefinitely, or tell the doctor I was unfit for
work.

It went on like this until the following afternoon, with her
coming regularly, either kind or menacing, which heated me more than
ever. I simply wanted to escape from my bedroom, without having
people in and out like clock-work, and was due soon for a holiday
anyway. I had been unable to eat or sleep for at least three days
and nights and, apart from the thermometer, the situation seemed
absurd and I was quite sorry for being a fairly unwitting cause of
this three-day upheaval. I knew an apology was the only way of
escape, but had no intention of making one. But eventually I was
almost in tears, and unexpectedly heard myself saying I was sorry.
She replied that she had always liked me, and always would, 'but
surely you don't need to be told so every five minutes' - as though
I had staged the whole thing for attention.

Anyway, it was over, and I still felt tied to my agreement to be
'loyal' if possible. I went to a brief staff-meeting that Sunday
afternoon in my dressing-gown, in a daze. Tommy was praised
publicly for the first time for her improved discipline, and was
more pleased than one would expect. In conclusion Mrs Strang said
that in future the staff-room would be vacated by 11 p.m., except
with her permission on special occasions such as Christmas Day.
Nobody said anything - it seemed a small thing to open and close the
quarrel. Next day I got up, feeling awful, and didn't do much work
that week. Mrs Strang had her usual anniversary party on 5 December
for her second year as Head, and I was on holiday. We were all
making an extra effort to be a big, happy family again.

About this time Anna felt the need to buy four goldfish in a
small aquarium, which she kept in the staff-room. Some of the staff
gave special interest to these fishes - it seemed simpler to conduct
a happy relationship with them than with some of our higher vertebrates (warm or cold bloody). Mrs Strang then bought four goldfish
for her upstairs sitting-room. I don't know whether the fish felt
smothered, but they did not thrive, upstairs or downstairs. Being
the farmer, it was my job to kill them when they reached the
suffering stage. Once I was sent for to execute Mrs Strang's
'Frilly-pants' - the only fish of hers I knew individually. Frilly,
having been at death's door, had suddenly perked up. 'She looks
better,' I said. 'Yes,' she replied, 'perhaps... but she must
go - no good being indecisive about these things!' This inability
to work for genuine health, or to recognize it when it comes, or to
forgive people unless they are quite broken down, is one of the
saddest features here.

CHAPTER 12

In mid-December, we had a visitation from the chief inspector, Miss
Florence. Mrs Strang was nervous about it and planned a full
programme beforehand. On arrival Miss Florence came straight to the
farm, and told me she was very pleased with the work we were doing
there (Mrs S later said I should feel highly flattered). After she
had looked round the other departments, they had a turkey lunch (one
of ours) with the committee. Then she heard the girls - trained by
Mrs Strang - sing. They do sing well. The last item was a Nativity
play produced, with some obstacles, by Anna. Mrs Strang received a
letter of thanks from Miss Florence, which seemed a bit ambiguous to
me, saying she was pleased with what she had seen 'and, as Headmistress, you will know how much of this is due to you'.
     That autumn there was threat of war in the world abroad. Having
found that the girls were even more ignorant than I of outside
affairs, and frightened by Mrs Strang's talk of war, not into the
better behaviour expected of them, but into a strong feeling that
their rightful place was back in their own homes, I attempted to
tell the farm-girls a bit of world news each morning as we milked
the cows. Mrs Briggs and Anna and I sent a joint letter to our MP
about the government's actions. This is not the sort of thing I
do - perhaps I just appreciated an opportunity to make a complaint
to somebody about something. The MP seemed a bit hurt in his reply.
I felt more sympathy for him when he was in the dog-house himself
soon afterwards, although I daresay the government's dog-house is
more dignified than ours.
     These and following weeks in Downcroft formed a period of uneasy
truce, while we tried to pretend everything was all right. I, since
the previous November, did little but work and keep quiet. Mrs
Strang seemed to be trying to protect Anna from me, and must still
have been agitating underneath. We went to bed obediently on the
dot of 11 p.m. at the latest. In an effort to stop 'talking',
Romany and Anna and I concentrated on other things when together.
We drew and painted, played 'Scrabble', listened to all kinds of
music, and started correspondence courses (mine in journalism).
Anna had asked Mrs Strang if we might all meet for discussion weekly
about 'the work' in general. Mrs S offered to answer any questions
we cared to submit. We produced a list of over forty questions,

covering many aspects of remedial treatment. She was clearly
nervous at these sessions, anxious to leave no loop-hole for general
discussion. We sat dumb and rapt to encourage her. She started
with mental illness as a comparatively safe subject, but the whole
thing soon petered out, and had only been a concession to the young
idealists on the staff.

Even Freckles, the original school cat, was quite different by
this time. She had been a proper cat, having kittens regularly, and
was part of the school, joining us often when the girls assembled,
taking her chance in a rough-house like the rest of us. After her
operation she grew fat, completely organized by Head and Deputy,
with liver in special dishes instead of kitchen scraps, and a 'night
toilet'. The girls are not allowed to touch her, and one feels she
is in at the top, perhaps not as happy as before. I think the girls
have grown to hate Freckles, though they are sentimental over
animals – it must be hard for them to see so much affection lavished
on a cat, who doesn't give two hoots, when they themselves need it
so much and receive so little. Mrs Strang thinks Freckles is an
expert judge of character: 'An animal always knows,' she says, when
Freckles bites a lowly resident. She brought Freckles to my room
when I had 'flu and she sat weightily at some length on my aching
legs. Later Mrs S told me, 'Freckles asks to go into Miss
Palethorpe's room – I had to force her into your room!' Freckles
has lived here since Downcroft opened, under three régimes; heaven
knows what it has seemed like to her – she can only live in her own
little world, like Tommy.

Christmas 19X7 was much as usual – quite happy but more tiring
than one realizes at the time. Head and Deputy had clearly
quarrelled briefly overnight, and Miss Palethorpe wore such a
thunderous-cum-beaten-dog expression at breakfast that it was
impossible to say 'Happy Christmas' to her. The farm-girls and I
enjoy the routine work on Christmas Day – it goes nicely between all
the food, and the cows wear paper hats from our crackers for
afternoon milking. In the late evening, remembering the staff were
allowed to stay up later, Mrs Strang organized a comb-band, and
accompanied us tirelessly on the piano, saying Anna played her comb
like a 'cello and I mine like a trumpet. I enjoyed Boxing Day
morning most – Anna and I found ourselves free after 11 a.m. and
asked to go out for an hour, though Mrs Strang was not pleased as it
is understood that we forfeit free time over bank holidays. We
returned for lunch in high spirits; whereupon Mrs Briggs remarked,
'You two have had a drink' (she always knows immediately from what
she calls my defiant twinkle) and Mrs Strang looked black. We paid
for our brief excursion later, as Mrs S told us we must take charge
for the evening because the upstairs trio had had no time off, and
she retired for an interrogation session.

At Christmas we seem to have too much to eat all at once. Our
food is usually good but necessarily unexciting, and we have the
extras all together – the girls are encouraged to stuff, while being
liable to be termed pigs. Until this Christmas, the girls liked
being able to offer us a toffee from their ration. I don't care for
sweets but used to accept them. This time we were overwhelmed,
partly because the girls received a lot from home. They began to
force sweets on us in great quantities and were unable to see that

one's liking for toffee has no connection with one's affection for
the giver. At this point Mrs Strang made a new rule that no girl
was to offer sweets to staff, although it was only a temporary
phase. The same evening she unearthed trouble among the farm-girls.
I sat in her room late while she interviewed them singly and
together, and wiped the floor with them. They had worked extra hard
contending with bad weather and poultry-trussing, and I hated to see
them so miserable - having their home-leaves 'postponed' for petty
trouble which had been much exaggerated. (Postponement is more
apparent than real, because Mrs S cannot bear to cancel an arrangement once it is made, so they do usually go on the specified day,
but don't expect to go until the last minute.) I remember Babs was
blasted with force because she had dreamt that she climbed a wall
into the outside world, this being taken as an intention or a wish
to abscond. I felt weakened by having to listen to the whole
degrading business without being able to say much, but knowing they
were tired as I was. In January I felt inwardly tearful at times.
     I don't usually make New Year resolutions, but made two for 19X8
because things seemed to be getting on top of me: first, to be
kinder to Hazard, our most temperamental cow. Both Hazard and
Heffalump go through unnecessary kicking phases, when I have to milk
them, quite frightened not only of their hind legs but that there is
no one else to turn to if they get beyond me. It was expedient to
bluster Heffalump into submission but it made Hazard worse, and I
had vented too much spleen on her at times - also the girl who
normally milks that cow takes it very personally if one is cross
with 'her cow'. I did keep this resolution from the beginning.
Whereas Hazard used to be afraid of me, she is now very attached
(she missed Harmony acutely) and she stays behind after milking to
put her head on my shoulder, which is unusual in a cow. Second, I
resolved to be more tidy - unfortunately I did not master this
before the worst happened. I am not fussily tidy by nature but have
to make efforts here, and we try to maintain an unnatural state of
cleanliness on the farm (in spite of Mrs Strang's muddy paths). The
girls are very untidy and no sooner are they trained than they have
to leave.
     I had got behind with the farm theory (there is a large and
varied syllabus for the UEI exams each March, with individual girls
at different stages), through missing our evening classes while I
had 'flu, holiday, then the Nativity play and Christmas, and now I
had only two evening classes per week instead of three. In January
I taught them in every available moment during the day and we
covered most of the syllabus by the end of the month. Also in
January Anna, Romany and I became very hungry. We had been without
a full-time cook for months, and the food was duller and skimpier
than ever before, especially in the evening. One would rush indoors
from a two-hour evening class for supper at 7.45, ready to go on
dormitory-duty at 8.15, but the girls were often sent upstairs at
8.00 p.m., so one had to bolt supper (i.e. dinner). Sometimes we
came in famished, to find the meal consisted of one limp square of
greyish-yellow Welsh Rarebit, followed by a greyish-yellow stewed
apple. For the first time we began to buy a little food of our own,
eating it in Romany's more isolated room on the top floor with music
before bed-time.

Towards the end of January my mother was ill, and it was arranged
as before that I should take leave for her convalescence - 2½ weeks
in February. Before going, I finally caught up with farm theory but
was behind with the practical work, and asked Romany to have a
general tidy-up while I was away. The day before I went, Mr Forbes
(committee) visited. Romany showed him round as I was teaching, and
she told him her sensible idea for altering the farm buildings in
order to enlarge our cowshed. I knew Mrs Strang would disapprove of
my assistant talking to a committee member, especially as she was
out of favour, but said nothing to Romany about it as she was a bit
unsettled already, with a less even temperament than first appeared
but good fun in between.

After a few days' leave I received an incoherent letter-card from
Anna, saying the situation was beyond her but she would tell me more
as soon as possible. I waited for a week on tenterhooks, though not
thinking it concerned me directly. Then I had a long letter,
sounding desperate, from Anna which she asked me to burn. She
explained partially, and I will add some details I learned later,
but the worst of it happened just before I returned, so I never
quite knew about that. Mr Forbes had telephoned Mrs Strang soon
after I went on leave, telling her tactlessly about Romany's idea
for altering the farm buildings. This caused an unpleasant staff-
meeting, when Romany was told to write out a complete account of her
conversation with Mr Forbes. Mrs Strang also met Mrs Pemberton in
Glebe that day (Mrs P had left, out of favour, about a year before)
and the latter told Mrs Strang that she and I would never get on
until we had 'had everything out' and that I was disloyal to her.
(A bit hard, after I had visited Mrs Pemberton, with whom I continue
friendly, specially the previous November to tell her I had decided
to say no more about Mrs S because of my abortive 'loyalty
agreement'.) Mrs Strang was wild. Meanwhile the same day, Romany
was extremely upset, cried most of the afternoon on the farm, wrote
out the required account of her conversation in the evening plus her
resignation, and handed both to Mrs Strang, still crying. I don't
suppose Romany ever intended the sequel, but Mrs S was unexpectedly
'kind' to her, and she blamed all her unsettlement on to me. She
made several criticisms of the way I manage the farm, and was also
resentful that I had not taught her to drive the tractor. Mrs
Strang went hot-foot to inspect the farm, professed to be shocked by
its disgusting state, raised cain, and took Anna (who had never seen
Mrs S so wild) to see it too.

Before I returned they re-organized the farm and got it into
'proper order'. Romany was now in great favour, and promised to
fill my post if I left suddenly through pique. Mrs S told her that,
even if I did not leave, she herself would visit the farm daily to
keep me up to scratch. Anna said in her letter that she didn't see
how I could possibly stay now. But I imagined we might get over
this phase, and was almost incapable of leaving by now anyway, and
was not going to be pushed unpleasantly. I knew all this before
returning, except that during the final weekend Mrs Strang had long
sessions with my colleagues individually and ferreted out all my
disloyalty over two years (though it had virtually stopped by the
previous November). It was hard to imagine her getting this
information from them, when I'd been on such good terms with all of

them, but they must have been convinced that I'd been very wrong.
And of course I knew it was wrong to 'talk', especially to new
staff, but did not see that we need be divided as a result. They
went very badly through the mill I imagine, and then were
'forgiven', upon certain conditions. But I did not know this latest
development until after my return.

On 22 February, I drove the 200-plus miles fast, being torn for
the first time about returning, and thinking there would still be
lambs and books and music, etc., whatever happened. I arrived at
5 p.m., and found no one about, except Romany who was obviously
nervous. I went up to my room, after Mrs Strang coldly handed me
the key, and found a sealed envelope on my dressing-table (a bad
sign) containing a list of twelve new rules about the farm. It was
on a long piece of paper, in block capitals with underlinings in red
ink, signed by Mrs S earlier that month. I won't bother to
reproduce it here, but there is a framed edition in the farm classroom to this day. Some of it was justified, other rules were
nonsense and almost impossible to keep without upsetting other
school rules. In any case I am supposed to be answerable to the
committee, not to Mrs S, for my running of the farm.

I drove straight over to the farm, in my first proper second-hand
car which I was beyond enjoying, while nobody was there, just to see
what standard of cleanliness was expected, so I would know for next
day. It did not look too impossibly clean. I saw several small
changes, and notices put up by Romany, and some interference with
the farm theory. Romany had also set up a seeds trial in the farm
office, to see whether I was justified in carelessly keeping the
remainder of last year's seeds, and I quite sympathized with these
seeds being put to a test they were unlikely to pass. I came back
indoors, unpacked, and had a longish bath with a cigarette, and then
found Mrs Strang knocking and listening outside my bedroom door. It
turned out later that they had been looking for me, and were afraid
I 'might do something desperate'. (It was a strange feeling to have
them all unfriendly suddenly, yet simultaneously anxious about me.
Suicide did cross my mind once within the next few weeks, but only
briefly and not seriously.) Mrs Strang asked coldly why I'd
returned a few hours earlier than expected; she also said my
presence would be required at a staff-meeting tomorrow lunch-time,
to decide amongst other things on a new site for the manure-heap!

I changed, and went down to supper, feeling a stranger. They
talked among themselves and, when I spoke once, Mrs Strang replied
unconnectedly about the recent worry having an adverse effect on her
stomach ulcers. I saw Anna twice very briefly – she was not
supposed to see me at all, and she warned me that more was to happen
tomorrow, adding that things might seem different on the surface
but ... but I couldn't hear the last bit, and took it that she
remained friendly irrespective of appearances. I went to bed at
about 9 p.m. Next morning it was a mere flea-bite to find that
there was no longer cooked breakfast for the staff because only I
wanted it, but much later my stomach used to feel like a vacuum
cleaner by lunch-time. We were all on tacit tenterhooks until the
staff-meeting at 1 p.m. – those present: Mrs Strang, Miss
Palethorpe, Miss Crandle, Anna, Tommy, Mrs Briggs, Romany and me.
After one or two opening remarks (no mention of manure) the main
business began, and seemed to last for an hour.

I think I've never known anything worse than that hour and the following months. The others told themselves later they were shaking like leaves. I can't remember it very clearly. Mrs Strang began by saying she understood I'd been worried for some time about things at Downcroft, that she was now going to clear it up once and for all, after which there was to be no further discussion or disloyalty. She dealt in order with the things I'd been reported as saying behind her back. First was 'sailing near the wind'. She went into this in detail (not realizing I meant her habit of taking either deliberate or impulsive unnecessary risks). She took it to mean the Punishment Book, which I had not mentioned as I never see it, though it is unlikely to be kept correctly when the punishments themselves are against official rules. At first I felt I would die if I'd been mistaken in what I'd said and had slandered her - it was bad enough even if I was right. As she continued, I knew that what I'd said was true, although she was making an excellent case for herself. Even I was almost convinced by her, and anybody new would have been convinced. Then she dealt with my talk of ex-colleagues 'leaving under a cloud'; she went through each one, giving her own easy-to-believe reasons for their leaving. Next came my statement about her 'having a bad influence on people'. She spoke in a tired, hurt way by now. She mentioned a long letter I'd received recently from Dorcas, which I'd shown to two colleagues, and asked whether I'd still got it? I croaked yes - the only time I spoke. She also said, embarrassingly, that apparently I considered myself responsible for her appointment, but she had enquired of the chairman who assured her I'd had nothing to do with it! (It transpired over a year later that she hadn't asked him.) It went on - perhaps about her hopes, fears, efforts and discouragements, and my disloyalty, ingratitude and her health - I don't know.

It stopped about 2 p.m. for afternoon work. I looked in the cloak-room mirror as I put my gum-boots on, and was surprised to see that my face looked fixed but much as usual, and my hair had not suddenly gone white like Marie Antoinette's. Romany was late in arriving at the farm because she was upset and had gone to Mrs Strang for sal volatile. We kept up appearances in front of the girls but didn't know how to look at each other. We got through the rest of the day somehow, except for an argument about which of us should see to a batch of day-old chicks at dusk. After I'd gone to bed early again, Mrs Strang apparently sent for Anna and Romany to ask for a report of my conduct. Romany said I was being difficult. I could understand the rest, but thought this the limit, when Romany must have known it was hellish already without her keeping on.

They half expected me to 'do something desperate', but the only desperate thing I could do was to keep going ordinarily, and I had insufficient strength for leaving anyway. Nights and meal-times were the worst, but I was determined to eat and sleep and not to be ill. I was quite devastated, having always loved the farm and my work and been far too attached to it, and having greatly enjoyed the friendship of the lower staff, and it seemed unbelievable that both should be turned upside-down simultaneously, and that real friends should be afraid to have anything to do with me. In a way it was strengthening and I should never mind so much again. I remember during the following weeks finding comfort in an egocentric way in the fact that the sun continued rising and setting, even though my little world was shattered.

It is difficult to describe the attitude of the staff, but the whole thing was humiliating, and uncomfortable all round. They were not allowed to speak to me except on essential work matters, so I was in a suburb of Coventry, and it was no use my approaching them because it was risky for them to approach me, and it went on for several months. The following day, 24 February, my bacon was partially saved because Mrs Strang heard there was to be a general inspection at the end of April, so had to be a little careful. That evening I was off duty and drove miles away to see outside friends. On return I found Romany singing loudly in the entrance hall, but she hastily re-arranged her face as for a death in the family. I snapped at the staff occasionally – mainly at Anna, as being the safest person. Mrs Strang did not come to inspect the farm daily, as she'd said she intended. By the 27 February she was agitating about the letter I'd received from Dorcas, and I was told via Anna to take it to her sitting-room. To my relief she put it on the fire without reading it. After that I went through all my belongings and burnt anything at all doubtful (letters from ex-colleagues, and disreputable working clothes which had been criticized for being unmended and untabbed, etc.) on the boiler fire. I cleaned the farm buildings myself the first few weeks, and then was too busy, and have kept up what I consider reasonable standards.

I had my first real talk with Anna a week after returning, and felt better. I really didn't know what to do, and was still dazed. I thought that as Mrs Strang had re-convinced the staff she was right, it must be left like that, until they saw for themselves. I wondered, very briefly, about changing posts with Romany and becoming farm assistant, but decided this was ridiculous. I had steered fairly clear of Mrs Strang for about a year, particularly since the previous November, and now it was a relief to be completely clear until I am leaving, eighteen months later. But at first I felt uncomfortable, as one has a natural impulse to apologize and be forgiven, and I did think it wrong to have 'talked'. But I knew it was best to say nothing, because she would have required a complete apology, and my admitting all I'd said was untrue, and then she would have been more powerful than ever. So I said nothing, and tried to be 'normal'. It was another twinge that Mrs Strang was being pathetic and talking of her stomach trouble, which I cannot help thinking she uses as a weapon for us and the girls. Miss Palethorpe wrote the minutes of the staff-meeting and we all signed.

It was awkward with Romany on the farm for several weeks, and not easy telling her what to do. She rarely agreed now when we discussed farm policy, and tended to appeal to Mrs Strang who interfered without any knowledge of farming, so after a bit I made my own decisions without talking it over with Romany. Soon after the beginning of March Mrs Strang was on holiday, but remained in close contact with the school. She sent a postcard to the down-stairs staff to say that she had had an idea after seeing the Pump Rooms in Bath. I said to Anna that perhaps she intended to build a special interrogation room at Downcroft, and Anna replied laughing, 'You must be feeling better to make such a good joke' (a doubtful

one in fact!) On the rare occasions I saw Mrs Strang, she
varied - sometimes harsh, sometimes like a harmless old sheep.
Sometimes she pretended to be frightened of me - she surely couldn't
have been really. If I went to her room on business she would go
through the motions of continuing work at her desk, while I, having
knocked beforehand, stood waiting. Then she would look to see who
it was, and jump, or look alarmed or half-cringe, which seemed
incredible. She still does it occasionally, or makes as if to stand
back for me to pass her on the stairs, when she knows I always stand
back, and I know she would kick me down the stairs for two pins.

On her return from leave later in March, she visited the farm,
and was most unreasonably rude, angry and critical, though I was
doing all I could. Afterwards she questioned me in the staff-room
in a most bullying manner, tied me in knots over the farm accounts
and estimates as though I were falsifying them, and left me reeling.
Later (and she must have done it for this purpose) she told Romany
and Anna that she had 'hauled Sparrow over the coals', and asked
them whether I had complained to them about it. Fortunately I
hadn't to any extent. I don't remember much about the rest of
March. For some time after the upheaval there seemed to be numerous
'knocks' (as the girls would say) in morning prayers about
disloyalty and stealing people's reputations, etc., but no doubt it
was a case of 'guilty conscience', as the girls would also say.
Actually the whole thing gave me such a jolt that I forgot about
being tired and was rapidly on top of the work again.

Looking back now, at the end of my time here, it seems extraordinary to have put up with events in November 19X7 and February
19X8 onwards for a moment, but it is hard to see clearly at the
time, and Mrs Strang is most expert in making you feel guilty, and
the girls are having similar experiences all the time, and there is
always the fact that you are expected to go on duty and keep up
appearances, and then there are plenty of enjoyable happenings on
the farm to lose myself in.

CHAPTER 13

The general inspection lasted for nearly a week in April. Anna had
by now recovered from her fear of talking with me, and it made all
the difference to have one person talking naturally. She and I
hoped that something would emerge as a result of the inspection.
Once here, one should really either agree and stay, or disagree and
leave. It is not much use trying to work in one's own way if the
atmosphere contradicts it as this produces further conflicts for the
girls (that sentence was the gist, omitting outrageous frills, of
Dorcas's burnt letter).

I hate the idea of making an official statement to the committee
or inspectorate, quite apart from being afraid of the resultant
unpleasantness. (I keep using the euphemism 'unpleasant' because it
comes from an old catch-phrase originating from Mrs Briggs: 'Things
is very unpleasant 'ere.') But it is equally distasteful to keep
quiet about ill-treatment which should be aired. The situation is
difficult to convey to outsiders, and one knows Mrs Strang has all
the answers, and has covered most contingencies beforehand. But to
'leave quietly' is just to avoid the issue, which is what I am about
to do, I think (writing in August 19X9).

We realize of course that the inspectors know a great deal more
than they appear to do, and are also in an awkward position.
Beforehand I decided not to go out of my way to make criticisms to
them, but to answer direct questions. I hoped Downcroft would be
running typically enough for them to see for themselves, or otherwise that they would see below the surface. Some colleagues were
nervous in anticipation, but Mrs Strang pretended it was only
inconvenient at its worst, and that we should not, of course, exert
ourselves to do things any differently. Two inspectors, Miss Merton
and Miss Amos (the former's senior, perhaps) were here the whole
week, staying at a nearby hotel, visiting daily. Others,
specifically to look at health, education, domestic economy, etc.
(except that my Mr Dean for the farm was off sick) came for a
separate day each during the week.

I don't know how it seemed to them, but it was odd to us, with
bits on stage for the audience and often fraught behind the scenes.
The inspectors were friendly to us all, but it was impossible to
relax, and we were all, including myself, infected by the desire to

94

keep up appearances. Presumably they are not really impressed by
the extra spit and polish prepared for their visits, except that
they are almost in physical danger of slipping. (We have an apt
line in a morning hymn: 'Let not my slippery footsteps fall.') We
pretended it was quite natural to have the upstairs trio in our
staff-room. Although I usually need to have the girls working hard
on the farm in the evenings, I put on a cattle-judging competition
one evening, and made rosettes for the girls to award to the cows,
and I took them on a rare visit to another local farm later in the
week (perhaps not altogether hypocritically, because we have a lot
of spontaneous amusement during ordinary working days on the farm,
and one cannot have mild horse-play under inspectors' noses, so it
was true enough to arrange a few enjoyable events). Our new cook,
Miss Curtis, only recently arrived - an enormously fat person, with
a vast expanse of white bib and tucker which she called 'my shelf',
a first-class cook, accustomed to working in Stately Homes
hitherto - was delightfully and unconsciously frank with the
inspectors, which I daresay they appreciated as a rare phenomenon.
    The girls soon realized that the inspectors treated them like
human beings, and had to be damped down between public appearances.
Mrs Strang was agog lest the girls be questioned, but I don't
imagine they were asked leading questions, or that they would have
dared to answer any, or even quite known how. Once or twice, after
I'd had a harmless chat with Misses Merton and Amos, Mrs Strang sent
immediately for me: 'I'd like to know exactly what's been said, Miss
Sparrow, then we shall all know where we stand.' Anna and I were
pleased by one early suggestion that we might each (those in charge
of a department) keep a monthly report book of our own girls'
progress, as this meant positive progress would be recognized, and
the system has continued since. As Mr Dean could not come, Miss
Merton (with whom I am largely on egg-selling terms during the four
years I've known her) discussed my work with me herself. Mrs Strang
kept coming into the room on the defensive. Miss Merton wondered
whether we should have a full-time man to do the routine slogging,
to free me to teach. I prefer us to do our own work, not least
because working together is the best chance for conversations, but
somehow to organize it to be less pressing. (My 'teaching', other
than in evening classes, is scrappy - for example, before we start
carting manure, which is 'dirt' to new girls, I spend ten minutes in
my classroom running through the nitrogen cycle. When I am tired, I
teach animal sex and reproduction, because the girls are always
silently fascinated by the subject.) I was very glad that Miss
Merton raised the subject of the changing population of farm-girls,
as I do want them to come and stay, without constantly being
threatened with removal for the slightest misdeed. Miss Merton
informed Mrs S.
    During the week Mrs Strang sometimes found it difficult to
maintain politeness; she found Miss Merton 'changeable', and Miss
Amos 'not as sensible as before'. One morning at breakfast, she
gave the girls a loud, rather crude lecture on their continuing
behaviour and discretion, and then was dumbfounded to find the
inspectors already sitting waiting for prayers in the entrance hall
when she came in in her lay-preacher's gown to take prayers, and she
was obviously fearful in case her blast had been overheard. This is

what I really mean by 'sailing near the wind' - a constant inability
to avoid taking quite unnecessary risks. The education inspector
suggested that some girls were capable of working for GCE, which was
inspiring for Anna. He also visited the farm classroom. It was
embarrassing when he and Miss Merton studied the large framed list
of Tidiness Orders, which I bitterly resent hanging in my department. He said, 'I suppose you and Mrs Strang put your heads
together over this?' I replied, 'Well, not exactly.'

They made several suggestions during the week, but a full report
would be sent several months later. If anything practical is
proposed to Mrs Strang, she seizes upon it with immediate gusto. We
were quickly immersed in plans for housework, GCE, evening classes,
room changes, etc. There was a new idea to simplify housework, with
virtually the whole school sharing routine work each morning before
separating into departments (an 'experiment' on which we were not
asked to comment, so it continues). It meant that Romany and I were
working alone on the farm the first part of each morning, and it is
more difficult to complete tasks. Anna was at a loose end before
schoolroom classes began, until Mrs Strang had the bright idea of
putting her 'on drains' - that is, supervising the meticulous
cleaning of drains all round the house daily - hardly economic use
of a trained teacher, though Anna managed to find interest and it
became a popular job with the girls. In comparison with exaggerated
surface-cleaning, the farm drainage system is extensive, and
requires frequent roddings through, but again it is fascinating to
deduce the underground life of Downcroft - for example, I can look
down a large inspection pit in a field and later mystify the house-
girls by knowing when they finished scrubbing.

We were also to have more cultural activities. Mrs Strang
reacted semi-sarcastically by drawing up an elaborate time-table
with anything remotely cultural clearly labelled 'CULT. ACT.' It
started several new activities and I gradually began a weekly art
class, but although staff and girls welcomed these innovations,
there was no reduction of other work. Another good idea was the
conversion of a small room for about six girls to use when nearing
discharge, for them to do their own small-scale cooking and
laundering. From late spring and off and on throughout the summer
this year, Romany was unsettled with her own private affairs, and
had several periods of sick leave (not pregnancy) which made her
easier towards me.

Just before Whitsuntide I heard from Maureen, a former farm-girl,
saying she was coming to stay at the Glebe hotel for Whit weekend,
specially to see us. (Maureen had been a difficult girl, but was
particularly fond of Mrs Strang and me. She had had no settled home
since being a month old. Currently she was on probation, after
stealing from two sets of local lodgings here, with condition of
residence in a London probation hostel, and was now proud to be
doing well. Earlier she attended out-patients at our local mental
hospital, and once, when employed on a nearby farm she turned up
here with a nail hammered into her stomach - she said it was an
accident but it seemed to have been done deliberately to attract our
attention, and she received scant sympathy. Recently a former
landlady of hers had been murdered for money, and it was at first
thought by the police that Maureen had done it, as there were

several points of similarity with the young woman who was actually
charged. It was just after this that Maureen wrote.) She regarded
us as her family, and had courage to rise to an hotel. I forgot to
tell Mrs Strang she was coming, but presumed she would be as welcome
as other old girls who occasionally call, with or without appointment.

While driving the van back to Downcroft on Whit Saturday
afternoon, I met Maureen unexpectedly nearby. She got into the van,
hardly able to speak, trembling violently. According to her, she
had just called at Downcroft, but was ordered off the premises by
Mrs Strang. I had a cigarette with her in the van, and said I might
be free after dormitory-duty in the evening and would meet her
outside her hotel to go for a drive in my car. I returned alone to
Downcroft, found Mrs S very het-up about Maureen's rudeness, though
she certainly came with the best of intentions. Mrs S was reluctant for me to meet Maureen at 9.30, but I said I must, not least
because Maureen planned to call here again next day, hoping to find
Mrs Strang softened overnight. Mrs S seemed to spin out dormitory
duty on purpose, so it was 9.45 before I reached the hotel to find
Maureen not there. I left a message saying I would try to come
again next morning, returned to Downcroft and put my car away.

Then I saw the vague shape of Maureen running back from the farm,
where she'd been looking for me. I went to meet her but she hid,
realizing she was not supposed to be in the grounds. I looked round
the bushes, saw Mrs S at her upper window, and withdrew into the
shadows. I went to the staff-room window to enlist Anna's help, but
saw Miss Palethorpe at the door, and crept away. I was beginning to
feel hunted myself, so was relieved when Maureen popped up from
behind a bush, and I hurried her off to my garage. It was creepy
down there, and seemed more so when Maureen said: 'I want to ask you
something - did they think I'd done that murder?' No wonder the
wretched girl needed to see us so badly. I drove around with her
for three-quarters of an hour while we talked. She was very hurt
about Mrs S but not exactly resentful. I got back at 11.15 to find
Mrs Strang waiting up for me accusingly. It was the first time I
had defied her openly since February! (Maureen's probation officer
later wrote a letter of complaint about her unhappy visit to her old
school.) Another ex-farm-girl visited us on Whit Sunday, without
Maureen's violent temperament, but smarmy and about to go to a Farm
Institute - she received a very different welcome.

After the general inspection Anna met Miss Amos occasionally in
London. She advised us a little over the next year or so, was
fairly frank and very kind. Evidently the inspectorate had some
idea of the picture and were concerned. They appreciated the fact
of Mrs Strang's hard work and that Downcroft has 'no outstanding
discipline problems' (so we were therefore admitting more disturbed
girls). They thought Mrs Strang has a very strait-laced conception
of good and evil, but things would have to change, and they thought
this was possible. Miss Amos said Mrs S lacks confidence and, as
changing would be a difficult task, we could help by supporting her
and showing that we had confidence, and 'finding some middle way of
compromise'. (Exactly how one can do this in the circumstances I
cannot altogether see. Since February I had felt conscience-
stricken about poking around for the mote in her eye. But to shut

one's eyes to her mote produces another variety of beam in one's own.) At this point I half-regretted having lost my position to give her the extra support necessary, but thought I might make a controlled effort if there really was any hope of things changing. Miss Amos thought it unwise for the staff to discuss amongst ourselves; if we were unable to bottle it up, we ought to talk to friends outside. I do agree and have virtually not done this since November 19X7 with anyone except Anna, which seems reasonable. I have often listened to what other colleagues think.

It had been slightly awkward with Romany on the farm all this time, and easier to get on with the work while she was on leave. She returned about the middle of June. I had leave in July, and heard from Anna that there was a lot of trouble with a group of girls, who had stolen money, etc. from locked drawers in staff bedrooms, and several had planned to abscond. Anna said the interrogations had been terrible, she would never forget Bessy when finished with. Mrs Strang seems ruthless in reaching what she calls 'the full truth', and an amazing amount comes out of what appears to be solid butter in the girls' mouths. But I doubt whether one can ever know definitely, when the girls have such a range of pressures put upon them, and are terrified into blaming each other wildly. Mrs S is often satisfied with findings which are clearly not 'fully bottomed'. She ignores facts which do not fit with her preconceived ideas, which is not even scientific. On this occasion for instance, she refused to listen to my explaining later that Bessy could not have stolen chewing-gum from my wardrobe because there was none anywhere in my room.

Anna wrote to say that early in July she, while chauffering Mrs Strang, had been questioned again, and had told Mrs S she did not agree with her methods. Anna also said that Romany had now completely changed in her attitude towards me, thinking I had been right, and very much regretting all that happened in February. On my return in mid-July, I told Romany I was glad, but that I still thought it had been wrong for me to 'talk' to new members of staff, especially to my assistant, and that I would rather not discuss things with her, but she could say what she liked to me. She seemed to think this was hedging, no doubt it was, only there was no need for me to change again suddenly just because she had. Anyway, we did not keep to this completely – often something was funny and it was most enjoyable to be able to laugh about it again. It is merciful really that Mrs S has an odd collection of 'funny little ways', peculiar and ha-ha (interspersed with those less amusing) and we tend to find relief in extracting the last drop of humour from them.

Another complication that summer was Mavis. She was difficult from the start, and we hardly knew what to try next when she failed in her farm job near Mardon. As she had a boy-friend there, it seemed expedient to find her factory work and digs in Mardon. Mrs Briggs and I searched for digs for a week before finding a second-rate landlady. Mrs S was impressed with Bob, the boy-friend, and hoped he would marry Mavis, but he was already married. Bob and his wife came here to ask permission to have Mavis to live with them. Mrs Briggs and I were sent to see their home and to tell Mavis she could live there. It was the first time I had met Bob, and I was surprised that Mrs Strang had been taken in by the glib sort of man who insists on trying to make you drink far more than you want. She is so ready to believe the worst usually. I felt sorry for Bob's timid little wife, completely under his thumb. The former landlady was appalled and said she would write to her solicitor. Mavis said 'I know plenty about her anyway', which I said was no way to go on, but Mrs Strang was interested in the landlady's skeleton. Official questions were asked, and the committee met about it. Mrs Strang (it appears to me) cleared herself this time by telling the Mardon probation officer how worried she was, and then wangling a letter of reassurance out of the PO which was useful to show our committee as its tone suggested Mrs Strang's doubts and the PO's harassed confidence. The situation blew over, with Mavis continuing to live with Bob for a time.

At the end of July I had been here for four years and felt depressed. Even the morning hymn on my anniversary was 'He that is down need fear no fall'. The same morning I heard that Mrs Strang considered me 'too pleasant lately', and wondered what I was up to. About the same time, she told Anna categorically that she and Romany and I were not to be together at all. It was maddening to me never to have any say in these phases, and never to know when a new one was due, and whether it would be better or worse. Simultaneously Mrs Strang was very angry with me, and criticized my supervision of Erica, who had boasted, perhaps unrealistically, of smoking comfrey on the farm. Nothing was said to me directly about the veto on meeting my two closest colleagues, but it was clear we were in another phase. As Anna's bedroom was above mine, I knocked on the ceiling that night (knocking with a tall book, while standing on a chair placed on my dressing-table) but descended so precipitately from my Heath Robinson elevation that I could not hear whether there was a reply, though assumed there was.

The following day we had a slightly nerve-racking staff-meeting, and in the evening a cousin of mine turned up unexpectedly. It was a strange evening - Anna and Romany and I were officially separated, it seemed, but kept up appearances, and my cousin thought all was well. After supper I received a message from Mrs Strang via Anna that I 'had been seen' to kiss my cousin on his arrival. Apparently the girls were unnecessarily agog, though nobody seemed to be around when he arrived. Soon after the message there were screams and a girl was put into detention. Mrs Strang later in passing, after the minor upheaval had quietened, said disgustedly, 'All because you kissed your cousin!' I replied quietly that it was a pity if we could not meet discreetly behind his car, and she snapped back, 'You can kiss the back of the car for all I care!' Really I thought it might come to that. Not that I am on kissing terms with anyone here now except Mrs Briggs, but we were with the girls in Miss Gracey's time.

Also about the same time there were difficulties with Erica and Mary. Erica was an unusually intelligent transfer, interested in farming. I was asked to help her take GCE Biology at 'O' level, but had only acquired textbooks and looked up two words from the syllabus in the dictionary when she absconded. The police removed her from the roof of a hospital and she was transferred to another school after a few weeks in a psychiatric hospital. At the same

time I went to fetch Mary from Slough as a recall. The evening
after Mary returned, at 7.00-7.30, I heard peals of hysterical
laughter in the girls' dining-room. It was so reminiscent of the
completely uncontrolled way in which they used to laugh at Miss
Gracey (an unmistakably flesh-creeping sound in a school such as
this) that I went near the door to see if help was needed, but it
sounded as though Mrs Strang was controlling the laughter herself
and (I supposed) encouraging them to laugh at one of their fellows,
as that is usually the cause of loud laughter here now - one tries
not to cause mass laughter oneself, because it is taken as a sign of
poor discipline.

Afterwards when we met for staff supper, I asked Mrs Strang what
the laughter had been about. She told me briefly that she had been
reading aloud to the girls some letters from Mary's boy-friend,
found in her suitcase on return. (We have to censor letters and
luggage, but I do think they should be kept as private as possible.)
I asked how Mary had taken it, and Mrs Strang said Mary had 'laughed
her bloomin' head off' with the rest. I said, 'I suppose that's all
she could do, poor thing!' 'WHAT did you say?' - Mrs S has a
disconcerting habit of asking one to repeat provocative remarks,
which are harder to say a second time. I repeated what I'd said,
omitting 'poor thing'. She said little, the meal started as other
colleagues joined us. One of them asked about the loud laughter;
Mrs Strang explained, and then turned on me. 'I suppose you didn't
like it! Mental cruelty or something like that, I suppose?' I said
weakly that it must have been embarrassing for Mary. She replied
most unpleasantly that I mustn't think Mary is as easily embarrassed
as I am - 'No doubt it would embarrass you to have your love letters
read out, but then, you're normal....' She must then have
remembered that she advertises me as not quite normal, so added
quickly 'to all intents and purposes!' Nobody spoke for a bit, and
my hands were shaking so I stopped eating for a few moments. One of
my colleagues gave me a gentle kick under the table, others gave
small looks of sympathy while the meal went on. (I may have had
some inkling then that she is truly bewildered in failing to grasp
the fact that the girls do have feelings.) Afterwards Miss Curtis,
our newish cook (who was in blissful ignorance, and cannot credit
the difference between her own size and mine, so referred to me as
'our little farmer') could not understand why I had been 'attacked'
in this way. Mrs Strang often takes the line that I must not think
others are as sensitive as I am, knowing this embarrasses me in
itself, but I only find her theory relevant when killing goldfish.

I told Mrs Strang that in mid-August Mrs Briggs would have been
here ten years, and she organized a dinner-party but no present.
(We give Mrs S a joint present each Christmas, birthday and
anniversary as Head.) Mrs Darby, as a former long-server, was
invited. Mrs Briggs was excited and determined to enjoy her
celebration. To our surprise, she stood up at the end of dinner to
make a speech. She spoke up with much feeling and concluded by
saying she must tell Mrs Strang how grateful she was to her for...
(we waited, breathless) ... 'clearing up the shocking vulgarity as
was in this school before she come!' (In fact Mrs Strang's interest
in sex is more offputting than any other underground sexual
activities here. Dorcas once said, 'We have masturbation for

breakfast, VD for lunch, constipation for tea, and homosexuality for
supper!' She is supposed to 'hate smut', but constantly says things
which others just don't say, or even know, and some of her beliefs
seem quite unfounded, such as perspiring hands being a sign of
masturbation. Girls are sometimes physically sick when she gives a
routine lecture on VD, and she sometimes perceives girls with
Hutchinson's teeth 'all covered in green slime', which I certainly
never have. Once, during a Sunday sermon, I was almost pleased when
she said the girls need not despise those of them who have been
adopted because they'd been chosen, but she added that even those of
them born in wedlock need not sit smugly, because 'you are probably
the product of unbridled sexual intercourse'.) After dinner Mrs
Briggs and Mrs Darby became more excited, talking of the old days.
I think Mrs S can hardly bear us to talk of the past here, though
she likes to hear a contrast painted between the former chaos and
our own sobriety.

There seemed to be a campaign after the general inspection to
make some link between Deputy (Miss Palethorpe) and staff. I think
we have been fairly willing, if not eager, but she shows so little
interest. She is more friendly when dependent on us during Mrs
Strang's holidays, but if she has to make a decision then she is
liable to go back on it later, without batting an eyelid. Mostly
she is unpopular, though I think several people blame her too
much - she is after all only the negress in the wood-pile. Mrs
Strang seems so uncertain herself that she needs someone who will
back her to the hilt, which implies that her Deputy is either having
a hellish inward conflict or stands to be badly hurt sooner or
later. Miss Palethorpe has become more like Mrs S, though more
feminine except for shouting unbearably at the girls, and has a gift
for repose, and a Victorian way of life almost, with girls to wait
on her hand and foot. She can be very rude to lesser members of
staff (only once to me), often in front of the girls. The Deputy's
post is delicate even in ordinary circumstances, but I suppose she
is simply a senior member of staff, and has some responsibility for
liaison. All Miss Palethorpe's loyalties are towards the Head,
which does not matter as we can manage. But I think some colleagues
do need help - they have problems, and in this sort of work we could
do with support sometimes.

Anyway, in the aftermath of the inspection, Miss Palethorpe asked
me to go out for lunch with her on her birthday, as it was my day
off. I don't think Miss P altogether dislikes me, although my
cultural conversation had run out before we returned. None of us
are much good at ordinary conversation any more - there are so many
forbidden subjects that it cannot flow naturally. It is amazing how
the girls still chatter, as there are even more banned topics for
them.

CHAPTER 14

Romany gave in her notice at the end of August 19X8, in order to leave at the end of October before a quiet wedding, which Anna and I attended. After my leave at the end of September, I returned to find there had been an explosion over Miss Curtis (marvellous cook) which had been brewing for some time. Miss C had taken to living in her kitchen mainly — I remember slipping in there one late evening to find her privately studying a book on Edible and Poisonous Fungi! By early October Mrs Strang discovered that Miss C had been discussing her views, both with girls and outside, in an exceptionally candid way. I think this was brought before the committee, one of whom had happened to sit behind Miss C on a bus and heard her give a lurid description of our Deputy and say that 'Miss Sparrow is the only lady on the staff'. There was a tense atmosphere within the school, which was assembled to be warned very strongly about gossiping with members of staff. Miss Curtis forestalled any further plans by handing in her notice, and she left soon afterwards, with her explosive feelings barely concealed under a dumbly dignified exterior, and artificial cherries bobbing defiantly on her best hat. She is now in clover as cook in another Stately Home — we had much enjoyed her cooking, and I think she could have settled here nicely with a bit of care.

The two applicants for the vacant post of farm assistant were a nineteen-year-old girl with some training, and a middle-aged Irishwoman with considerable practical experience. This would be my ninth assistant, including several earlier part-timers (some not mentioned in my diary) so I had no very strong feelings about their suitability, and felt the older one would be better able to look after herself, so I plumped for her and the committee agreed, having enquired whether I would mind having an assistant so much older than myself. Also Mrs Strang had 'a stop in her mind', a 'feeling' against the younger (apparently innocuous) one, 'and my feelings are never wrong, so I shall not ignore them again'. I had told her briefly that I intended to be 'more sensible' with my next assistant, which is the nearest I ever came to making an apology after February and, though she followed me agog for further recantations, I added not a word. Romany and I had quite a happy last month together on the farm; both she and Miss Curtis had added

a bit of colourful life to the staff-room. About mid-October a
woman (later known to be Miss Sidebottom) stayed in Downcroft
overnight. By a feat of organization, none of us met her, but we
heard later that she would be coming as the new cook in December.

We heard that the inspectors were coming to make their report to
the committee at the end of October. On the Sunday beforehand Mrs
Strang sent for me, told me I was looking pale and strained, that
there was no need for it, and it must stop. She went on to ask what
possible cause could there be for my appearance and manner? I
thought she was actually asking, and muttered something about a
rather difficult summer. She replied that I had no difficulties
whatsoever, was not having to work so hard as in the past, and had
had a capable assistant in Romany - 'at least you've always said
she's very capable?' 'Yes.' 'Well, that's that then, and there's
no need for you to look as you sometimes do.' She went on to say
that she expected complete discretion from me with the two new
members when they came, and that Miss Sidebottom is extremely
efficient - 'I'm not saying quite as efficient as Miss Crandle, but
nearly.' And that in future she intended to spend more time in our
staff-room, mainly at tea-time, and would expect politeness there
from me: 'You are the main reason why I stopped coming to the staff
sitting-room.'

In this and other ways, she prepared for her day of judgment, but
was extremely het-up on the day, especially when the chief inspector
plus regional superior (Mr Findley, the one who was 'poorly after
the riot') and Misses Amos and Merton turned up in a body to make
their report to the meeting, at which Mrs Strang was present part of
the time. Anna poured tea for them all afterwards in their meeting-
room, and was given challenging encouragement by the chief, Miss
Florence, which we recite frequently to each other as it emerged in
blank verse:

Take courage!
You have a sense of humour - use it
You have a lot to give - give it
                    No matter what!

I did not expect to see them (as we do not feature at committee
meetings) and had got wet on the farm, was tired with attending to
two cows who calved during the previous night, and had quite
forgotten (I think not with malice aforethought) about trying not to
look strained, so my appearance with hair in wet rats-tails must
have been at its worst. But they came briefly to see me in the
staff-room, and Miss Florence's greeting was less inspiring: 'Have
you had 'flu?' (there being a horrid epidemic at the time). I think
I answered, 'No, have you?' Mrs Strang looked sheathed daggers in
the background, and Miss Merton said that she herself tried to
mother me and to give advice about my leisure (which I am well able
to enjoy on my own initiative in fact) and Miss Florence expressed
pleasure over my art class. I drove them to the station, and
overheard Mr Findley advising Mrs Strang in a final word to be more
relaxed herself.

After they had gone, Mrs Strang was over-excited and larger than
life, saying repeatedly: 'We're wonderful! Do you realize, we're
wonderful!' It was hard to understand. I imagine they sugared the
pill, and she was probably too agitated to digest anything but the

sugar, and has no gastric troubles in her mind as distinct from her
stomach. Apparently the inspectors, in between praise, had made two
criticisms, (a) about the girls bringing up the rear of the church
congregation without meeting local people; (b) that too many bells
ring during the school day. Mrs Strang treated these minor points
with the slight irony they deserved. From the number of practical
changes we saw, both before and after, it was clear that more had
been said. It seemed later that there was a written report; that
the committee resented some of the criticisms and planned a
complaint to the inspectorate. Altogether it was confusing. The
girls were told that inspectors and committee were so very satisfied
that they had decided to make this an Experimental School - our 'new
methods' would then be tried elsewhere if proved successful,
depending on our girls' full co-operation meanwhile. There was a
good deal of surface shuffling but no real change.

As Romany left, her successor arrived - a Peter Pan Irishwoman,
whom we call Paddy, with extra-stormy likes and dislikes for various
people. She lay low initially. In my usual little introductory
talk, I said that although she is experienced she would have to find
her bearings on our farm, so it is wisest to keep quiet until she
found her feet - then the girls wouldn't know which way she was
going to jump until she was ready to jump; also that I have a bit of
fun with the farm girls when we feel like it, but it was better for
her not to do so until she had gained their respect. She says now
that she was in a whirl the first week but has learned rapidly
since. But although a very hard worker, her wild temperament proves
a problem both with girls and staff. I often feel, perhaps
unrealistically, that some of our really odd and awkward 'downstairs
staff' would seem much more normal in a different environment.

Anna saw Miss Amos in London again in November. We gathered that
Mrs Strang was being encouraged gently but firmly to change her
methods. Anna herself was thinking of leaving, and of taking
further postgraduate training for social work. Miss Amos said she'd
been horrified by my appearance (at its worst on their recent
visit), and that she thought I should leave. She suggested that our
replacements might be less long-suffering than we, and this would
provide further inducement for Mrs Strang to change, if she were
ever to keep her staff. Anna had decided to leave the following
July 19X9 when her GCE group had sat their exams, but I would not
consider leaving, especially if there were any hope of change,
except that I might 'in a year or two' after gathering the necessary
strength. Mrs Strang had another go at Anna about now, but made
little headway. Anna and I very occasionally disagreed about my
firmer attitude with the girls, and my method of leaving them free
so long as they are basically under my thumb on the farm. (For
example, Anna questioned my irritation with Beryl for blowing
bubbles in the dairy. But although I blow bubbles sometimes in my
own bath, when taking lengthy baths for the sake of evading Mrs S on
her war-path days, Anna may not realize how difficult it is to sell
milk up to the required standard of purity, when the girls seem to
think I have DTs while I try to explain that millions of bacteria
can dance on a pin-head.)

In November I had a sudden urge to see Dorcas, whom I had not met
since the day she left here (in April 19X6) and I thought Anna would

enjoy meeting her too. The inevitable subterfuge leading to such a
meeting went, for once, like clockwork, and we set off on the early
evening of 21 November in high spirits, to meet Dorcas at an hotel
for dinner, halfway between London and Glebe. However, we hardly
noticed the excellent meal (including pheasant), and it was a shock
to find Dorcas still at fever pitch about Downcroft, even though she
was here only a few months, 2½ years before. She did not ask what
had happened since, but fired away with her stimulating capacity for
making startling truths which still remain after you have discounted
the outrageous exaggerations surrounding them. Her theme was that
she felt deeply ashamed to have been at Downcroft at all, and
doubted whether she would 'ever feel clean again'. I sat miserably
(with a black eye, where a farm girl had accidentally tapped me with
a drain-rod, and been terrified it would be reported by a prefect as
deliberate attack) thinking that in that case I was already doomed
like Lady Macbeth. Dorcas continued hotly for about three hours;
Anna had already decided to leave, and I tried to state my case for
staying. Amongst many other things, Dorcas said that, no matter how
hard one tries, one is bound to lose integrity on Downcroft's staff.
Her main example was the way in which Pearl had been stopped from
making with me what was believed to be 'her first personal
relationship'. Finally I said, 'You'll probably say something
caustic, but I really feel a little improved in some ways!' (not
having had to struggle similarly before coming here). Dorcas gave
her Mona Lisa smile, and we parted on a slightly gentler note. I
found it almost impossible to accept that one had automatically lost
integrity years ago, simply by staying, when one could be
comparatively 'happy' here, were it not for the struggle to preserve
what one had imagined was integrity. I protested to Anna during
most of the drive home again, though knowing it was wishful
thinking.
     The next day we had to concentrate on our first Open Day, when I
had assumed we would literally be open all day to anybody. However,
we didn't know till near the time whether we were invited ourselves,
and it turned out that only the common-room plus small exhibition
(of sewing, etc., not misbehaviour) was open for about two hours to
about twenty Friends of the School, including committee. The girls,
conducted by Mrs Strang, sang well. Miss Palethorpe sang with them
because the altos had been purged beforehand. A friend of mine came
with her mother, who prides herself on a flair for 'reading
character in the face'. She saw much positive in our girls' faces
while they sang. 'But there's one girl', she whispered to her
daughter, 'much older than the rest - she must have come back time
after time and it only needs a glance to see why - I've seldom seen
a more sullen or vicious face....' 'Hush, mother - that's the
Deputy!' 'Oh no, my dear, I mean the one in the back row., they
would never have her as Deputy....' 'She is the Deputy, and middle-
aged, and what's more has smartened up a lot recently.' I murmured
polite nothings to the Friends of Downcroft and passed cups of tea,
while inwardly battling over whether to leave.
     It came over me all of a sudden while I was lighting the boiler
fire first thing the next morning, and I decided to leave.
Immediately afterwards I milked Highlight (Harmony's last calf) -
the gentlest cow, whom we imagine creates poetry while gazing

vacantly into space, and my tears were running discreetly down her
flank into the bucket of milk. (If girls or colleagues noticed any
sign of dried tears, they would merely suppose I was in worse
'trouble' than usual, and I did feel to be, though not for the usual
reason of Mrs Strang's wrath.) I had no idea what to do next, and
thought all day - ideally I wanted something that hardly exists:
farming combined with proper social work. It is not easy always to
secure another post from here, and in any case I hardly wanted the
horrid conglomeration of my reputation to accompany me elsewhere.
In the evening, driving back from a visit to an old college friend,
I suddenly knew the answer, having assumed earlier that I was too
old and qualified to merit another course, but now seeing it was the
best way of starting again. Anna was away for the weekend, but
relieved when I told her my decision, which was to be kept quiet
until I had got a bit further with plans. It looked as though we
might both be students again.

Soon after, it was Mrs Strang's third anniversary as Head.
Beforehand I made my usual gesture for the day (i.e. a grandiose
cartoon) - I did not like to stop giving her one, but it seemed
silly to continue, so I solved it (?) by drawing something that
could be taken either way. The picture showed all the ingredients
of our Experimental School (girls, staff, animals, manure and all)
moving round the border until the standardized, butter-wouldn't-
melt-in-the-mouth product emerged on its way back into the outside
world in the top centre; while in the middle stood our Head,
perilously wielding her sledge-hammer. At the last minute, I
thought she could hardly fail to see its meaning, but it was almost
sad, if a relief, that she didn't. We had our usual celebratory
dinner on 5 December, at which Mr and Mrs French gave some easement.

As part of the Experiment, the girls were to have mass home-leave
for ten days in December, leaving just a small group of new or ill-
behaved girls behind. This had been used as a lever for weeks, and
the girls were on tenterhooks. The staff were to have mass leave
too, leaving Mrs Briggs, Tommy, Paddy (my new assistant) and me
behind to look after nine girls, and I was to be 'nominally in
charge'. Apparently there was official criticism later that the
upper trio had all gone on leave simultaneously, and I was hastily
made Number 4 on the staff, but was not told directly of this small
promotion. Everything was planned in great detail for the exodus,
with some rooms in use and others sealed off (including all rooms
containing documents and belongings of the Head) and we were
suddenly on our own. Mrs Briggs was lost in a cold, and had two
difficult girls, upset by a last-minute shout of 'great, fat slobs';
Tommy had two girls for housework and laundry; Paddy and I had four
on the farm (two useful, two very dim and difficult). A ninth girl
was due out of hospital.

We all quite enjoyed our ten days together though there was
little let-up. Four staff sounds plenty for nine girls for ten days
but there was an unusual amount of work still to be done, and the
farm buildings were being altered (Romany's 'legacy'). We worked
hard during the day and had peaceful evenings, with volunteers
rather than sticking to set duties. In the evenings I played games
with the girls, listened to their favourite records, and helped them
to make Christmas cards. We had one or two small upsets, largely

through prefects, but Tommy said it was the first time for years
that she'd been without nervous aches and pains. The girls wrote
letters home which I had to censor - several seized the chance to
try to sort out their family relationships. One wrote, 'Please
please have me home for just a little time please'; another wrote to
the wrong divorced parent and received a scathing reply - I didn't
give Cilla this letter until Mrs Strang had seen it, but she thought
'it would do Cilla good'. Molly, who was trailing about each day
carting coke and coal in frost and fog, wrote home to say it was
heaven, and that we were living a life of 'pease and lucksury'. I
also enjoyed receiving my mail each day at first hand, and seized
the opportunity to write to several Universities about social work
training while the replies could be received privately. It was
ironic to be more trusted again at this point as 'Number 4,
nominally in charge'.

When the ten days were up, I spent much of the day fetching girls
and staff back from railway stations until tea-time. It was
organized chaos in the evening. Rows of sullen, homesick faces.
Rows of carrier-bags in the entrance hall, waiting for the Customs.
Miss Crandle and I were on our knees, looking for contraband in the
carrier-bags. Then followed one of the events one can hardly
believe one has seen. Mrs Strang lost her temper, and began
throwing girls' shoes through the doorway, to or at the girls. Miss
Palethorpe was slow to move, and at least two shoes hit her legs.
She was like a wounded animal at bay and turned an outraged look on
Mrs Strang. I said good-bye to Pease and Lucksury, and bent low
over a carrier-bag.

In the midst of this scene Miss Sidebottom (pronounced
Siddyba-tome) arrived in a most extraordinary manner - our first
introduction to her as our new cook who had been interviewed earlier
without our clapping eyes on her. How Mrs Strang could have pre-
viewed her as highly efficient is hard to say: the rest of us (who
would have to live alongside) saw her eccentricity in a split
second. She let a moth-eaten old cat out of its basket and
reassured it with a chorus of 'Diddums darling, there's a precious
girl - come and kiss me, my presh...'. I said, 'What is her name?'
'Diddums Siddyba-tome!' Tommy's face was a study, and I turned
round briefly to my carrier-bag again. Of course the cat's owner's
name gave scope for nick-names from girls, however it was
pronounced. Before the evening was out, we were dazed with her
volubility, and she proved a sore trial for at least the next year.
I grew to like her from a distance for her sheer outrageousness.
She and Paddy are complete opposites, both openly determined to be
different, so what with other staff temperaments there have been
clashes ever since, with numerous permutations and little peace in
the staff-room. Whatever other difficulties there have been in the
past, this is a new development - it seemed Mrs Strang's long-drawn-
out anglings to divide us had now been achieved with a vengeance.
There is no need to describe the tensions and constant little
battles, but it is a very real factor from now on.

We managed to enjoy the Downcroft Christmas routine without too
much unpleasantness. As usual, I heard from numerous people I
shouldn't have heard from (old girls and ex-colleagues) but was
virtually beyond minding. I also had a sudden urge to see Miss

Gracey again, and this proved possible for about half an hour while
she was passing through Glebe, without her being able to call at
Downcroft of course, though she writes of thinking about it daily.
It was disturbing to meet her again, after three years, and to see
the difference between the two Heads, and to know this one had been
dismissed. She did not want to talk about the present régime,
except to ask one question arising out of what she must have heard
elsewhere: 'Do the ends justify the means?' I.e. (as I can never
quite distinguish between means and ends) 'Are the girls settling
all right after they leave?' Again it was strange to realize that
she hoped I would say yes; she wanted the best - one becomes so used
to the other. I could not answer her clearly, though any vague ends
can hardly be justified by our methods. I have a feeling that the
ex-Gracey girls understood more later, when the confusing experience
was over, and that some were helped more than was apparent at the
time. But as all of them seem to need to see something good on
looking back, irrespective of the treatment they received in either
reign, it is hard to know.
      There was quite a lot of trouble after the mass home-leave -
several girls had planned not to return, and after Christmas their
behaviour deteriorated typically for January, February, March, which
must seem a long, grey, cold time to the girls. Mrs Strang was very
withdrawn during these months, either away on holiday or mostly in
bed on the premises without our knowing whether she was on or off
duty.
      On hearing my nebulous plans, my father thought me unnecessarily
apprehensive - 'You've been talking among yourselves and got wind
up', which is truer than he realizes. He wanted me to seek
promotion in another similar school, but one has been enough. He
insisted I do things properly, which meant approaching a top person
to request guidance. Eventually I agreed to ask for an interview
with Miss Amos in London, on 8 January - my day off, and she left it
to me to decide whether I would tell Mrs Strang beforehand. I did
not, still having no real plans, and she being even less approachable than usual. But she knew later of my secret trip, perhaps
through another inspector who would have preferred me to seek her
own advice. Anyway, it was a helpful day in London, with several
suggestions of jobs, courses or secondment, plus an interview with a
supremely important person (I only realized months later, especially
as I had a brief muscular spasm on the sole of my foot when seeing
her, and was concentrating on not kicking and hopping around her
room). They said they thought I am 'too sensitive' for psychiatric
social work, which is what I most want to do in order to understand
more, and that I might be better in Probation. I just thought,
without saying so, heaven help me if I were so sensitive as they
seem to think, though their warmth of concern was encouraging. It
was this week that Anna decided to return to Barchester University
for further study. We'd decided to hand in our notices as soon as
possible, though not leaving simultaneously, partly because our
joint resignations might give food for thought. In fact I think Mrs
Strang put a construction on our leaving together which we had not
anticipated ourselves.
      On 12 January I was on dormitory-duty when Anna came to say Mrs
Strang wished to see me to fix future leave dates. I explained to

her that I didn't think I would be here after mid-September. She
was startled, but quickly regained composure, and I gave her my
letter of resignation. She asked whether I'd be prepared to overlap
with a successor, perhaps without salary, and I said yes. By this
time she was excited, went to tell Miss Palethorpe, and then Anna,
saying I was 'wise to leave, rising thirty and likely to be thirty-
five before re-established elsewhere, and Sparrow's wasted here'.
(But I need not have been.) Anna said she knew, and would be
leaving herself at the end of July. Then Mrs Strang was quite
over-excited - she would obviously be relieved to have us gone but
the going might not look too good to the committee. She asked us
not to tell the rest of the staff until after the next committee
meeting.

Anna was currently producing a school play, based on a gently
humorous fairy story, and the next day Mrs Strang brought the date
of production forward to an inconvenient extent and in general
demonstrated that things were going to be awkward. I was supposed
to be making the props and some costumes, and went to ask Mrs S's
permission to do so, and to make programmes with my art class, and
for about £1 to spend on it. She scoffed, saying we could not be
hindered by the girls helping - 'We must be practical about the
matter!' (fodder for another catch phrase). We almost argued about
one or two other things; she enquired what exactly do I understand
by my Saturday evenings 'on duty by Arrangement'? I replied that I
never have understood, but simply wait weekly for an Arrangement to
be made. But it was an exaggeration for her to tell Anna that I'd
spoken as though she were 'a fiend'.

I was still unsure about which course of training to try for, and
had mixed feelings about continuing under the same central
government department or accepting their money for further training.
Normally I'm on the uncritical side, and came into 'The Work' with
every faith in it. Clearly the inspectorate have a difficult task,
and are organized to advise rather than impose, and have to
compromise a good deal and face criticism, and they know conditions
often are not ideal and try always to improve things. But I cannot
help wondering whether these schools are the best answer. It is
almost impossible to measure what a school achieves, and it is
disquieting that Downcroft on the surface must appear to be running
as smoothly and efficiently as any (we see the others on our
travels, especially when taking transfers). I suppose, at its
lowest, these schools (a) provide material needs for girls at a
vulnerable age, and (b) training for earning a living and running a
home, and (c) ease the public conscience by 'giving a chance' to
delinquent girls. At its highest, such a school could provide the
beginnings of a happy relationship with Neighbours and Self. In
fact I see no justification for plucking a girl out of her natural
environment and placing her in this artificial setting unless she
really will be helped here in her personal relationships. If a
school has the Downcroft attitude towards relationships, being
dangerous and dirty, I think many of its inmates would be better off
in the streets.

Anyway, I had an informal interview at Barchester University
later in January and decided to apply there, as there was not the
same difficulty about references and testimonials, being slightly

known of already through Anna. They accepted me without any
references, but may be getting a pig in a poke because I feel I
shall lose the self I know best on leaving here. A tutor in another
University gave me a useful tip: that, if it proves awkward to
explain lack of references or poor ones to future potential
employers, it is not in my interests to plead a bitchy referee in my
background, because strangers cannot know whether I or my former
Head are out of step. Another revelation about this time was that
Anna's former Barchester tutor advised her to have one discussion
with a London psychotherapist, in order to gain a little more
insight as to how best to cope with other people akin to Mrs
Strang - I had thought she was completely unique, and that we should
not meet her like again. A third revelation was at my formal
interview at Barchester, quite enjoyable, when the professor asked
me something about 'pecking orders', a phenomenon I've observed in
our hens (and higher vertebrates here) but it appears there is
theoretical knowledge of it in the social sciences. From last
December onwards I have saved every possible penny, having been
prodigal until then, to supplement a grant, and have now got about
£300. I took to chewing-gum and smoked fewer cigarettes, having the
idea put into my head when Bessy earlier had been unable to steal
non-existent chewing-gum from my wardrobe. On one occasion, I made
a single piece of gum last for six weeks; an old college friend
said, 'Well, I call that real thrift!'

CHAPTER 15

In late January 19X9 I had leave to stay with this same old friend
and her new baby for a week, and returned to Downcroft one tea-time.
I saw a number of girls on the lawn in deepish snow, shouting and
screaming, and could only think it was a small riot, so began rather
slowly to walk over to them. Anna came to meet me, explaining that
Mrs Strang had let loose a loyal group of girls to give 'a good
going-over' to a few difficult new girls, far-outnumbered. It was
half-pretended to be fun perhaps, but in fact was sickening. One or
two new girls put up a strong fight but mostly they were terrified
and one had a nose-bleed. The snow-fight stopped for tea, just
after I arrived. There was an entry in our communal farm diary next
day: 'Some of us taught Wendy C a lesson in the snow, ha ha!' (and
absurd too that they are not officially allowed to pinpoint their
less subtle jokes by writing 'Ha ha!')
    Apart from the cruelty and hypocrisy of this sort of thing, it is
just not safe when the girls tend to get uncontrollably rough. The
method is not used explicitly, but Mrs Strang sometimes puts a case
to the school in such a way as to arouse much righteous anger. I
remember in the autumn of 19X7 that two girls absconded one Sunday
after lunch. There were few staff in the place - Miss Crandle rang
the police, while I supervised the bulk of girls in their dining-
room. Two prefects unexpectedly caught the two absconders and
brought them to our door. Some of the girls were wild and had
planned to bash up the absconders - Kay, followed by others, rushed
to the door. I managed to get there before them, and struggled
between the two sides for a few moments, getting a slightly strained
wrist before shutting the door to separate the opponents. I think
this was reported to the Head later but she ignored it, although it
seemed more important than some of the trivialities she investi-
gates.
    These last nine months have been difficult on the farm, as I
rarely have a day off without one or two farm-girls being rude to my
assistant Paddy, and being removed from the farm either for a short
time or several times or permanently. I am virtually never
consulted and find changes whenever I come back on duty. There has
never again been a stable group of semi-skilled girls so it was hard
to accomplish anything. During these last months we have lost 20-25

girls. I could only speak indirectly to the girls and try to
influence Paddy, but she cannot see and it is impossible to say much
when the whole system goes contrariwise. Paddy was often shocked by
the girls' ingratitude 'when Mrs Strang is so good to them'. She is
the sort of person who boasts of having 'been brought up the hard
way' herself without it having harmed her. Often the girls are far
more tolerant and humorous towards her than vice versa. For
instance, she moralized in a shocked way when June said she had been
in detention no fewer than fourteen times. 'Well,' argued June, 'I
had to go somewhere for my summer holidays!'

After Miss Sidebottom's arrival we began to have very formal
staff-meetings weekly after lunch. We sat round a long table, each
with a typed agenda, and had minutes. We were to think beforehand
of anything we wished to raise, and hand it to the secretary, in the
form of one single word. It was rather like a word game - upon your
word being reached, you attempted to explain, and were often
squashed. Miss Sidebottom once put six words, and was squashed as
many times in rapid succession, and stopped playing. I felt like
putting (a) weather (may we discuss it?) (b) noses (may we blow
them?). Mrs Strang usually started the meeting in bad humour but
became elated towards the end if it had gone smoothly. At this
stage she began to read the records of new girls to us, perhaps
summing up: 'Yes, as I told you, a nasty piece of work - we must all
be vigilant. I wonder why they always refer the girls needing
strict discipline to Downcroft!' I still think the girls appreciate
one side of her - she can breeze them along and be quite amusing in
her snap decisions.

It was hectic before the play (produced by Anna against great
odds and purges) but this did brighten the winter. The final
performance could be called a howling success. The audience laughed
so much at this gentle play (one man's chair fell over with
laughter) that the girls' acting degenerated into slapstick. Mrs
Strang soon damped girls and audience at the end, saying we had not
invited them to pick their pockets, but that it would cost £80 for
us to have a proper stage. After the play, the rest of February and
March seemed quite stale - unlike any period before or since.
Everyone seemed too tired and hopeless to do much (even quarrel)
except work automatically. One of the punishments has grown to be
the writing of lines. 'I must not be clever' (i.e. not think I know
better than my elders); 'I must not puff, sigh or tut when I am
corrected' - preferably something requiring just over a line. Here
there was inflation too, though the downstairs staff tend not to
give lines. A thousand lines, for someone semi-literate with little
free time, is a lot. It was common for girls to have 5,000 or even
10,000 lines for a single misdeed, perhaps standing up to write
them. I once heard 50,000 lines threatened for 'dumb insolence'.
Occasionally (before inflation stifled them) lines were cancelled by
special dispensation, for example if an inspection was due. Running
parallel with this was Anna's difficulty in being allowed sufficient
paper for her schoolroom work.

In March we were busy as usual with exams (external) in farm,
garden and domestic work. In addition Miss Palethorpe entered a
large number for an external scripture exam, for which they had to
learn a few passages by heart. In March, after the usual time-lag

caused by Christmas, and then the play, I asked my farm-girls to concentrate. 'But you don't understand, Miss Sparrow, I've got 6,000 lines to write...' or 'But I must learn my scripture - if I don't know it I'll have to write it out X number of times.' So it was no use worrying them any further and most of them did as much as they could without being asked.

On 25 March I was rude to Miss Palethorpe. In the morning, Mr Gaunt, a dear old Baptist minister in Glebe, came to invigilate the scripture exam, and I believe there was some cheating under his Christian eye. It was my break-duty mid-morning, and I understood half the school would be missing for the exam. Break-duty is complex even normally - it lasts 15 minutes and one has to ensure all are present, punctual, toileted, STed, fed without dropping crumbs; that tables are cleared and wiped, and girls dismissed again on the dot into their departments. To my surprise this time, Mr Gaunt's girls turned up in dribs and drabs, disorganizing the routine. However, one is used to not knowing what is happening, and to picking up indirect clues from the girls, so I picked up and organized fairly adequately. Then Miss Palethorpe appeared in the doorway behind me, 'WHAT IS GOING ON HERE?' in a great shout.

I think this was the first time that Miss Palethorpe had undermined me in front of the girls, and I had promised myself a small retaliation if it ever happened, on behalf of many colleagues I saw suffer similarly. So I said, with airy 'politeness', 'I'm afraid I have no idea what is going on - I imagined you and Mr Gaunt knew.' She tried to stare me out with a dreadful face, so I turned round again to the girls, waited for her to take over or disappear and, when she still stood rooted, I started to give more orders as we were pressed for time. Miss Palethorpe contradicted the order loudly, and stalked off to complain to Mrs Strang, who then caught me with an angry blast. Miss Palethorpe subsequently was unusually nice to me for a couple of days, but as soon as I responded a bit extra for reconciliation, she was again hardly on speaking terms.

The same day as my half-enjoyable rudeness, we received a new staff-meeting book with some up-to-date remarks in it. There were eight new points but I will just reproduce four of them here:

24. 3. X9   There are one or two things which appeared in the beginning of the old Staff Meeting Book which I think we have all forgotten. As there will not be a staff-meeting this week, I think it best for me to list them....

III   The staff sitting-room and dining-room are for the use of all staff. We must remember that the girls can hear what is being said if voices are raised, especially against a wireless already playing somewhat loudly, and so can the HM above. A common-room must not have its privileges abused. Freedom of the individual is not licence to express one's feelings at the expense of other folks! (Her exclamation mark.)...

VI   I think it wiser to avoid politics and religion in staff-room discussions. Perhaps I should have said this under III.

VII   Farm-girls are getting later and later with meals in spite of 2 bells. Will all staff please see that all departments

are punctual....
(Signed by Mrs Strang)

Anna and I discussed this briefly together, rather than with other
colleagues. It was written more reasonably than sometimes, and
perhaps some of it did not apply directly to us, so at first we were
tempted to let it go. But we did not see why Mrs Strang should
continually write to us from just upstairs without getting a reply.
We hastily composed a reply the same evening, and put it on her desk
(a few points here, as above):

III   We have tried to keep the wireless quiet since this was
      raised (ill-phrased) at a recent staff meeting, and agree it
      is annoying to be able to hear it upstairs. We do realize
      the implications in the phrase 'freedom of the individual'
      ....

VI   We must use our discretion in discussing matters in the
      staff-room which are not connected with Downcroft. It would
      be wiser if we can manage ourselves to pour oil on any
      discussion which becomes unduly troubled....

VII   At the moment, while the cows are sleeping in, it is just
      possible with a rush to reach the house before the final
      breakfast bell. If anything goes wrong on the farm it is
      hardly possible. Once the cows are sleeping out again,
      which won't be long now, we shall manage more easily.
Anna Herrison
J. Sparrow

Then we waited, on slight tenterhooks. Mrs S found it late in the
evening and rushed into our staff-room with it, not realizing she
had no need to air it publicly. Four of us were present: Anna,
Paddy, me, and Mrs Briggs (who escaped immediately). Mrs Strang
stabbed her finger on point VI, saying we'd missed the point, and
there was no need for oil-pouring because the discussions were
simply not to start. Then Paddy, quite out of her depth but ripe
for a row and resenting the comments in the staff-book, voiced her
strong opinions about 'people who tell tales and people who listen
to them'. The difference between Paddy, and Anna and me, is that
the former lets everything fly in a row, and (obvious to Mrs S) has
no qualms about who hears, and she almost enjoys it. Also she
believes that if you 'are straight and do an honest day's work' you
need not fear man or beast. So Mrs S interrupted her loudly,
saying, 'Get up to my office, and mind you keep your voice down
too.' Off went Paddy, looking very militant. She returned, after
we'd heard raised voices aloft, still with her Irish blood up, but
highly elated and satisfied - 'I emptied me stomach!' I felt
apprehensive for her simplicity in being largely unaware of
duplicity, but then none of us are a match. I believe Mrs S quite
fears Paddy rampant - she knows Anna's and my scruples.
   I returned from brief leave in early April, and again felt a
stranger. The uses to which downstairs rooms are put change
constantly, and this time Mrs S had switched all the staff-room
furniture without prior notice, and had put a hard wooden chair in
place of 'my' dear old arm-chair, which was vaguely supposed by Mrs
Briggs to be the most important chair in the room, because the very
first Head had sometimes sat in it. The staff were annoyed but
helpless, and I've sat as comfortably as possible in a stiff chair

for nearly five months now. Mrs Strang summoned me on return to ask whether I had told the girls I am leaving. I had not, but it had apparently leaked out both from a farm-employer and from an indiscreet colleague. The girls were said to be agog, so were assembled and told officially that I am being replaced by a graduate and Anna by a gentleman. I think the girls were forbidden to discuss it and so made mainly veiled references, and anyway July and September were (to them) a long way off. I went up to the dormitories that evening to see the girls after my leave. Della, a temporary Communist, was reading invisibly in bed behind a book with a very large Capitalist skull depicted on the front. She peeped out over the top of it. 'Oh, it is you, Della,' I said, 'I thought you'd got very thin and pale.' As Della has a plump red face, we all laughed, not immoderately, whereupon Miss Palethorpe shrieked from afar about the noise.

Easter 19X9 was not pleasant and there were constant upsets between some other colleagues – Tommy was so upset by Miss Sidebottom that I think she spent every spare minute crying in her bedroom the next few days. Paddy had hopes of making an RC of me; I told her the most I would do was attend a service with her sometime, so she was excited when I found myself free on Good Friday morning (not the best day for initiation) and very keen that the only RC girl and I should do everything properly. I came back, changed into work-clothes, and then Miss Sidebottom asked me to drive her to our parish church of England for half an hour of the three-hour service. Rather than make two journeys, I asked if she would mind if I accompanied her to the service in breeches, and on the way there I happened to say I'd just been to the RC church. She was appalled, and seemed nauseated by my proximity, still warm from popery. On the way home she talked heatedly, distrait. Ever since March she has been saying, 'Of course we mustn't discuss religion and politics, and I think it's so wise, but it isn't discussing when I just tell you....' I told her now that I am not interested in politics and prefer not to discuss religion, but feel perfectly free to do so, or to attend services of any denomination.

We worked on Easter Monday, spending most of the day on the farm rodding through blocked drains. June said one inspection pit smelt just like the sea at her own home town. We decided to breathe deeply as the drains were our nearest approach to the sea that day. The previous Easter, Romany and I had painted an individual picture for each girl on a hard-boiled egg; the girls were reluctant to eat them, and some kept the shells in their bras (their best hiding place) for weeks afterwards, so Mrs S forbade decorated eggs in future. The girls have occasional day-trips but tend to go in a smallish party nowadays with extra spending money and treats, to make the ill-behaved girls (and staff members) who are left behind feel jealous enough to see the error of their ways. It is a little nerve-racking staying behind on these days because the remaining girls are resentful at first but later pretend they've had a lovely, peaceful day.

Things happened thick and fast all May. Anna, in early May, had an interview in London about a grant and, as her fare was paid and it was my day off, we both went cheaply on half fare. It was a hot day, and we kept sitting in parks and looking at ducks. We were

treated to lunch by Miss Amos (inspector). She had little to say
about Downcroft; nor had we in the circumstances but she remained
concerned for our futures. If no grant was forthcoming for me,
apparently it was still possible to study on full salary if I could
make up my mind to return to 'The Work'; she said I need not look
specifically for a farming post but could go in another capacity and
develop that side, say by keeping backyard rabbits (or bees in my
bonnet, I thought). She irritated me once or twice during the meal,
and I glanced under the table to locate her leg. This made Anna
slightly uneasy, as she knows I have a new game (akin to 'poor man's
polo') of locating vertebrate legs under dining-tables instead of
actually kicking these very legs, and she is half afraid my foot may
slip one day. In the evening we met Dorcas briefly for a meal, and
were able to enjoy it more this time. She had semi-apologized, in a
letter, for talking so heatedly about integrity before, but said she
slept better for knowing I was leaving.

It must have been soon after this that Paddy had violent words
with Miss Sidebottom and went to complain to Mrs Strang. Paddy had
a favourable reception: this was just what Mrs S wished to know – if
only the staff would tell her their troubles, then she could help.
Paddy felt that her own straight approach resulted in Mrs S eating
out of her hand. By now, the kitchen-girls were very strung up with
Miss Sidebottom; Paddy found a kitchen-girl, Sylvia, crying
desperately, and after much coaxing Sylvia said, 'It's nothing but a
living death in that kitchen.' Paddy reported this to Mrs S, and
again thought her kindness itself, even though Sylvia was put into
detention 'to think things over' after refusing to expand her
statement. Paddy seemed quite unaware that her interference had not
helped – in fact Sylvia was heavily punished, and we were told at
the next staff-meeting that it had been necessary to make an example
of her, as she was behind all the trouble in the kitchen, and had
made false allegations.

That staff-meeting (the last to which I was invited) began like
any other. But Miss Sidebottom said there was an unpleasant
atmosphere in the staff-room and she must know the reason why. Long
silence, with Mrs S asking for frankness. Eventually somebody had
to say something, and Anna said tactfully, 'We hear too much about
the kitchen', putting it mildly. Paddy jumped in heatedly but was
soon speechless to find the tables had been turned on her – that Mrs
S was on Miss Sidebottom's siddy, so to speak, and Mrs Briggs had
also changed sides after egging Paddy on for weeks. Then Mrs S said
that I had not yet spoken, seeming determined that I should. During
a longish silence, I racked my brains to see what could be said, and
suddenly heard myself say: 'All we want is peace!' Anna said
afterwards that she had nearly cried on hearing that, and Tommy said
she had nearly jumped on the table to clap and cheer. All that
actually happened was a short laugh from Mrs S, saying didn't we all
want peace. I was embarrassed for her as she went on to say that it
should be unnecessary to ask, but she did need our co-operation,
that her health is far from good, and worry is the worst thing for
it. Miss Sidebottom replied that she personally was very
sorry – 'You can rely on my loyalty and co-operation'. The
atmosphere was extra strained afterwards – Paddy boiled, Tommy was
scared, and Mrs Briggs 'kept her own countenance'. Miss Sidebottom

gave Anna a long private homily, saying she was shocked and grieved
by her remark (not Anna's own complaint in fact) but would forgive
her as part of her Christian duty. She (Siddy) added that she
couldn't understand Anna's distrustful attitude to Mrs Strang
(mentioned to her by the latter); she herself, she said, had found
Mrs S's methods a little perplexing to start with, but she had asked
Mrs Strang in a frank manner and been entirely satisfied with the
answers, and knew now that we could not be blessed by a more honest,
straightforward headmistress.

Not surprisingly, the girls were in poor form, and there was
unrest throughout the school. For some time they had been
threatened about their mass home-leave in August. Mrs Strang must
have realized the girls' atmosphere was serious, and one Friday
afternoon in mid-May she called an emergency meeting of the whole
school. All the staff were present, including Mr Marsh and Bill,
sitting in a long tense line at the back, while the girls sat in
rigid rows before us, cross-legged on the floor. Then Mrs Strang
stalked in for a dreadfully degrading scene. Much of her speech was
about relationships between staff and certain girls, and of how she
would not 'have a repeat of the Miss Curtis affair' (gossip).
Various girls were made to stand up to be verbally slaughtered in
public. At one point, when Paddy disagreed about a girl, she began,
'May I just say....' 'No, you may not' (in a great shout) 'I am the
headmistress of this school....'

Finally it appeared that two farm-girls, Sandra and June, who had
never seemed close, had been reported by a prefect 'to have touched
each other' - I am almost sure only to the extent of a hand on the
shoulder in passing, and really nobody except Head and Deputy dare
touch anybody. The two of them stood up to meet the accusation, and
were told that they could stand in the entrance hall that evening
for half an hour in public with their arms round each other 'and see
if that sickens you'. I could not believe she seriously intended
such an impossible thing. We all sat immobile. When Mrs S ordered
the school to stand, Lynette (fairly new) fell to the ground,
perhaps with cramp and emotion. One or two of us would have moved
to her, but Mrs Strang ordered us to leave her, and the assembly was
dismissed in silence.

Anna decided immediately to see Mr French (committee chairman).
She had already intended to see him before leaving, but now felt it
urgent. I said, not very enthusiastically, that I would go with
her, but she preferred to go alone. I said anyway she could speak
as from us both. It took an evening or two before she found him at
home, but it was sometime that weekend. Meanwhile I was on
dormitory duty the same evening (Mrs S was in bed) and wanted to see
what became of Sandra and June. They were sent out of supper into
the hall, and stood by the wall with arms folded, looking numb and
strained. I was quite helpless to protect them, but gave them a
smile of encouragement in their obstinacy as I passed by for
dormitory duty. Miss Palethorpe approached them, stared silently
for a few moments and then said, 'Well, you'd better get on with it,
hadn't you?' They made no answer or movement, and I (going very
slowly upstairs) applauded them inwardly. More staring. 'Or have
you decided it isn't such a good idea?' Miss P did not know quite
what to do. She left them. They came up to bed later, silent and

shaken. I think Mrs Strang said they must do it later, when she
came on duty, but I heard no more. Anna and I half felt we should
tackle Mrs S about this at the time, but it was too much on top of
Mr French.

Anna gave Mr French as clear an account of Downcroft as possible.
He was nice, but taken aback. It is of course hard to believe the
whole picture, but we both understate if anything. One interesting
thing was that he did not know of incidents which he had, according
to Mrs S, expressed an opinion on. He said he didn't care for Mrs
Strang and had known a certain amount but not as much as this. He
didn't want our final months to be too uncomfortable, but said he
would bring this knowledge to the committee meeting a few days
hence, and would we be prepared to answer questions at the meeting,
as Mrs Strang would either have to change or leave. (I forgot to
say that just before this, when grants seemed most elusive, Mrs
Strang was asked to give 'a confidential report' to the County
Council on Anna and me. She didn't mention it to me, but was quite
threatening to Anna – a sort of tacit blackmail as she was
particularly needing support then over staff conflicts. But we did
not worry about what she might say.)

We had to wait four days for the committee meeting. It was grim
waiting, but we were almost unable to discuss it, and had little
plan of what to say. There was the feeling that something would
happen at last, and that it had gone too far to do anything except
try to meet whatever happened. Anna was much more single-minded
about it than I was. I intended to rise to the occasion, but could
only steel myself at all by thinking of how much damage she does to
so many people, instead of my remembering her early months here. It
is quite extraordinarily difficult to tackle Mrs Strang. She is
like some mythical creature in that you nearly burst yourself to
grasp her nettle, only to find she has turned into a snake or a
humble worm or a crushed violet – which brings you not only
frustration but a sickening sense of shock. You never know which
side of her will meet your attempt or what strategy she will devise
or what repercussions will result, and she makes so much more noise
about it than other people, and is so open in her pain.

We knew it would be a sticky committee meeting anyway as
apparently the conflicts between Paddy, Miss Sidebottom and Co. were
to be discussed. During the day before the meeting Mr French came
to see Mrs Strang, was with her for some time but, judging from her
manner after, it seemed nothing very much had been said. On the day
itself, the thought of the meeting kept coming over us in waves. We
sat silently in the staff-room, not having confided in any other
colleagues. All I know is that, on one of my many visits to the
cloakroom before the committee arrived, Mrs Strang must have been in
the inner room, and I momentarily misread the label on the lavatory
door as 'ENRAGED' rather than 'ENGAGED'. The meeting started and we
waited, expecting to be sent for. The meeting ended and still
nothing had happened. In the evening I went over to a Farm
Institute to see if there might be a job there for Paddy, who was
expecting the sack and pretended not to give a damn. Later that
evening, Mrs Strang, fairly ominously, told Paddy she would wish to
see her the following day at 5 p.m., and Anna at 5.30.

That next day was my day off, and I told Anna I would return by

5 p.m., in case she needed support. But there was an unexpected
staff-meeting at lunch-time, with one or two outbursts between Miss
Sidebottom and Paddy and Mrs Briggs. Mrs Strang foresaw the
possibility of the whole staff knowing Anna had seen Mr French, so
asked her to make her criticisms public. Anna said she had nothing
to say at a staff-meeting, but was prepared to talk further to the
committee. Her 5.30 interview was quickly over as there was little
left to say. Paddy was highly elated after her interview. She had
told Mrs Strang she almost expected to be sacked, but Mrs S had been
surprised, and very kind and understanding, saying, 'I like you and
Miss Palethorpe likes you, and Miss Crandle likes you.' It is
pathetic since then that Paddy really thinks they do like her. So
now she was most relieved and settled in her mind. There was
nothing I could say to disturb this. I was half glad if only she
could stay happy, but feel she cannot for long. She spoke as though
the three of us had been through a very difficult time, but now it
was all safely over with the happiest possible result. So Anna and
I went out for a drink!
    The following weekend Anna called to see Mr French to ask what
had happened. He was still nice, but you feel like a poor relation
on these occasions: that you embarrass and discomfort people. When
he came to see Mrs Strang the day before the meeting, he repeated as
much of what Anna had told him as he could remember. Apparently Mrs
S set his mind at rest. So he had not felt it necessary to report
to the committee, and the whole thing was a fiasco. Naturally he
would not look for trouble, and Mrs S would quite easily convince
him. It must be difficult for the committee to know what to believe
about Downcroft, and apparently they prefer to behave like
ostriches. It is their responsibility mainly, and at least he has
been told our viewpoint. We could only think it apt that Mr French
had an operation for a literally weak knee - also his nice-ness is a
disadvantage to him.
    Things continued almost the same as before on the surface. It
was not extra unpleasant for me, because Mrs Strang continued her
policy for the last eighteen months of ignoring me to my face. I
imagine she knows from Mr French that I agree with what Anna told
him. I heard indirectly that I alone had been criticized at that
committee meeting for my 'disloyal attitude with the girls'. This
unwise familiarity between lower staff and girls is becoming more
common nowadays, but it is the one mistake I am sure of not having
made. All that the girls know, without words, is that I am
basically 'with them', which is surely what we are meant to be, and
it helps rather than hinders one's daily discipline of them.

CHAPTER 16

There is not a lot more to say. This is where my account tails off
in a way, though for me the climax comes nearer as each day
passes - the day of my leaving, which I dread. If I prolong my
diary now, it is only to delay the inevitable break, and to feel I
continue part of this place.

During the first fortnight in June I attended an introductory
course, on weekday mornings, at Barchester University (over thirty
miles away). It made a bridge for my next step but felt strange,
only unexpectedly pleasant to be a student again and not to have to
keep order, and to find ordinary discussion was actually encouraged.
In many ways, Mrs Strang was extremely careful towards Anna and me
during our last months, and punctilious in covering herself over
things like time off which we mind less about anyway. Occasionally
she could not control herself, or we caught strong looks of dislike,
but there was little contact and she was mostly coldly polite. So
was I, I suppose.

What with setbacks on the farm and so on, I felt unusually tired
towards the end of June. On 19 June Anna and I were sent together,
sharing the driving, to bring Cissie back from a failed job on the
east coast - about 400 miles. We left at 5.30 a.m. and got back at
11 p.m., with various small adventures in between, without Cissie,
who had disappeared after an episode with a carving knife. The
police (with whom we searched for an hour or so) were surprised that
Mrs Strang had warned Cissie of our coming. It became agonizing to
sit on the passenger seat of the new, bigger van. We had a poor
reception from Mrs S on our return but were too far gone to be
affable ourselves. She said we must both be off duty the following
morning because we had interviews with the County Council about
grants.

Next day I felt weak. Mrs Strang came to my room early to say
Cissie had been picked up and taken to a remand home, so I could
fetch her the following day with Tommy. I was too dazed to say
anything but that we must have a cushion for the passenger seat.
Anna and I put on our best clothes and set off like old women, not
enjoying the movement of driving, for our interviews - which were
delayed, and I could hardly climb the county hall steps a second
time. We were given hope of grants of £200 each, nearly half of

which would be needed for tuition fees. Anna asked if she could
share the next day's driving but was told it was most important for
her to have her day off. So Tommy and I went, over 400 miles again,
and brought Cissie back, with me driving very fast both ways, and
another poor reception, in that I was ordered to take the following
day as my day off for that week, which was inconvenient to me during
hay-making. I have said little so far about hay-making, but it is
an annual highlight when the girls, however non-rural, seem to
capture a primitive spirit of peasant forebears, so they are in
extra high spirits which I don't always share if the weather is
capricious.

It was now just before the GCE examination - Anna and her small
group had worked against heavy odds, not least in being despised for
'working on their backsides'. During the day when Anna and I were
away driving to the east coast, and the following week, Mrs Strang
had many private questioning sessions with the GCE group, singly and
together apparently, and began to settle her score with
Anna - doubly unfortunate just before the exam. These girls were
clearly brighter than most, and had probably never thought so deeply
or widely before, which was perhaps undesirable in Downcroft. I
cannot go into it in detail, partly because we knew little detail
ourselves; there had been a few petty incidents which Anna had dealt
with at her own discretion (and she was termed 'salacious', in
having let them read a book such as 'Woman of Rome') but she was
told nothing until the 'matter had been fully bottomed' with her
exam-nervy group who were forgiven by Mrs S towards the end of her
investigation. Mr French was fully informed.

Early in July we heard suddenly that Anna's mother had collapsed
with a serious breakdown. She was due to leave here anyway at the
end of July, and it suited Mrs Strang that she should take leave of
absence immediately to be with her mother, so she had virtually
finished. The girls were told of the illness, a bit as though it
were a judgment, and that Miss Herrison would require no meals until
further notice. They seemed to have grown more attached as the time
for our leaving grew nearer, and it was rather overwhelming when I
suddenly had to carry it for both of us - even those less personally
hit by Anna's departure did not want to be left out. I also
expected to have the concentration of Mrs Strang's dislike of both
of us during my final two months, but it was not quite like that.
She made a few tentative overtures to me during my final weeks - as
if to say 'All can be as it was now Herrison's gone', but the most I
could manage in return was cool politeness (which may be my own
weapon, as it can be a terribly dividing thing) and we continued on
a vague working basis of agreeing to disagree.

This summer we knew even less of what was happening - numerous
girls left without trace fore or aft from my angle, and no good-
byes. We also miss all sorts of spontaneous pleasures which would
endear an unaccustomed rural life to them, such as picnics. in the
hay-field, blackberrying, roasting chestnuts, picking primroses,
carol-singing round the neighbours - we are always busy and the
question does not arise. Officially the staff recently are even
more cut off from the girls. When they are on holiday or discharged
I find gradually that their letters and postcards do not invariably
reach me, and then they are hurt not to receive a reply.

Mrs Strang has tended from the start to use the girls' homes as a lever, which I think criminal, when even normally far more could be done to help family relationships, knowing they have been a source of unrest all the way along. Many girls necessarily become hardened at Downcroft, but remain extremely sensitive about home, and this may be the only line left for attack. It seems she has used this more lately, judging by letters girls have shown me. They are usually made to include accounts of misdeeds in letters home, and the Head sometimes writes herself, which upsets some families. Such letters are misleading, and the parents might be amazed to see how submissive their daughters actually are. Recently I am constantly having girls tell me things of this sort: 'I'm in trouble'; 'I've had my home-leave stopped'; 'They aren't going to write no more'; 'If I don't keep out of trouble they won't have me home.' It is hard to know what to say in reply, and the girl assumes she is in the wrong. Another pathetic aspect is that neither party has adequate words to express feelings on paper. I have read this type of letter, shown to me by worried girls, from their homes recently: 'When your mum got the letter she cried and fell on the floor you will kill her if you go on like this', and 'I will not writ again untill I get a good report, your everloving Mum xxxxxxxxxx.'

During the end of June and early July we were hay-making later than usual - the worst year ever, even apart from capricious weather. Paddy was what she calls high-sterical, would only work with certain girls and her own pitchfork, upset other girls and almost made herself ill. After much moil and toil we stacked it, but it heated through her determination to tread it too tightly, and we had to turn it all out again, dry it, and re-stack it in a heat-wave in thunderous silence, close to having strong words. (One bright spot was the staff's discovery in our local newspaper that Miss Sidebottom had been fined for riding a bicycle without lights after dusk. She was not amused, had hoped Mrs Strang might pull strings on her behalf, was fearful of our knowing - especially the girls, though they might have liked her better for it, were they not permanently exasperated by her now. She might have got away with it, Bill Evans told me, had she been less high-handed with the policeman who caught her, though he had numerous free drinks apparently on the strength of the story of his encounter.) Mr Marsh was temporarily less friendly - he had considered himself a kindred spirit of Anna's but now said our hair would stand on end if we knew half of what Mrs Strang was saying about us. He thinks he is the one superior person who paddles his canoe in a straight course, though in practice he zig-zigs (always kindly) as much as any of us.

The girls were thrilled to hear Anna was returning for two days to pack her belongings towards the end of July. An entry in the communal farm diary said: 'Miss Herrison comes back today Hip haray.' (I forgot to say that Mrs Strang found and used at least two of the girls' private diaries, containing frank remarks about their likes and dislikes for various members of staff, as part of her investigation of the GCE group. It gets quite nerve-racking writing my own diary in my bedroom sometimes, with footsteps coming and going outside my door, but I have managed undetected so far and have nearly finished. I think about it during the day while doing manual work and then write as fast as possible after 9.30 p.m.)

Anna packed quickly, and we had one or two jaunts to see outside
friends. At break-time on 24 July she was given her official
leaving present of a book token (so was I later). The girls were
allowed to carry her luggage to her car, but it became increasingly
difficult for her to speak to any of them though they seized every
opportunity. Miss Palethorpe was especially vigilant, roughly
interrupting those who tried to dally. On 25 July Anna was leaving
finally after breakfast. I was off duty, and went with her the
first twenty miles in my own car, partly as a dress rehearsal for my
own leaving. It all happened very quickly - she said good-bye to
the staff at breakfast, then to the girls in their dining room (many
crying); then handed in her keys at the office, and was given, she
said, a long level look and a crushing 'straight to the last'
handshake by Mrs Strang. We drove quickly down the front drive, and
stopped for a cigarette at the bottom. There is something (to me)
terribly final and death-like about this last going down the drive,
because you are cut off with limited good-will, and are unlikely
ever to go up it again. We had coffee together in a village, and
then went our separate ways.

I returned to Downcroft at break-time - nearly all the staff were
there plus Mrs Strang. People who leave under a cloud might have
died in disgraceful circumstances - all trace is quickly cleared
away and their names rarely mentioned openly. But some of the staff
and many girls had something to say privately. The farm diary said,
'Best woman on the staff gone', and Vi added that Holly, her
favourite cow, was in 'a bad mood and flaming temper'. After break
Mrs Briggs and I went for a little drive in the sun. ''Ere,' she
said, 'that was a funny job the way Miss 'Errison went, wasn't it?'
But she agreed she knew the pattern. She was really upset, seeing
her own retirement approaching before she feels ready for it, and we
agreed to write something privately in the book bought with Anna's
token, as it had no mention of wishes in it. Mrs Briggs said, 'And
with my permission you can put Happy Memories.'

That same evening I was on duty in the first-floor bathroom, with
a group of girls, including Della in the ex-GCE group (Della, the
self-styled Communist, with whom we were supposed to forbid any talk
of Communism whatsoever, but as it is her main preoccupation at
present one has to listen to a fair amount of gibberish about the
bourgeoisie and proletariat). Somebody asked permission to ask me
whether I had cried when I said good-bye to Miss Herrison, and I
answered (truly) no. Someone else said there was really no need to
cry because it was the best thing for Miss Herrison herself to
leave. Della asked if she could ask a question: 'What is it that
makes people like you and Miss Herrison ruin your lives to help
people like us?' I, taken aback, said something fairly incoherent,
'Well, for one thing we don't ruin our lives, we've been very happy
with you - I don't know that we have helped, you've helped us - and
as for "people like you", you're the best bit....' Chorus of 'Do
you really mean it? You've helped us more. How have we helped
you?' etc. Della returned to say, 'I'd better warn you, now Miss
Herrison's gone I shall have to depend on you quite a bit', and
departed to bed with a sweet smile.

I did most of my packing over the next weekend, and put various
keep-sakes the girls had requested in my waste-paper basket - an

excellent, if ungracious, place for distribution. I was away for a
week's leave in early August, and then returned for the final month,
when Paddy was on leave in Ireland. On my return, I found half the
school had gone on mass leave - the date had been kept secret,
nobody was about, the staff-room door was roped shut, so I went up
to my room to await events. Head and Deputy were later at their
most unwelcoming but eased slightly after a few days. The cows were
dotted extensively over the far field when I went out at dusk for my
usual last round of the farm, but must have scented me on the
breeze, as I found them gathered at the gate to give a most touching
welcome.

During this last month we adapted to the halved numbers by
working straight through from 7.30 a.m. to high tea at 5 p.m. I had
seven girls on the farm but they changed almost daily and two went
to farm jobs I knew nothing of, so it was impossible for me to leave
a skilled group for my successor. The remaining staff were Head,
Deputy, Mrs Briggs, Miss Sidebottom and me - we had meals together
at a separate table in the girls' dining-room, and the latter three
of us used the staff dining-room as a sitting-room. The meals were
not pleasant, and I had almost forgotten how unappetizing they can
be when we are together as a staff. Some of the sparse conversation
revolved round Mrs Strang's plans to build a new detention block
with three cells. The worst part of the meals was that Miss
Sidebottom was so much out of favour, and did not understand it.
She was snubbed by Head and Deputy in an incredibly rude way almost
every time she opened her mouth, and she opened it a great deal,
perhaps thinking it a 'mark of breeding' to pretend nothing was
wrong.

As Miss Siddy persevered, it grew worse. She still has great
admiration for the Head, but thinks 'she is overtired with worry
over the beastly girls'. Now Mrs Strang has so clearly removed her
patronage, Siddy has a worse time with the girls, who have grown to
hate her. She changed in appearance, and now looks ill, over-
wrought, and has hysterical bouts of weeping. She still thinks my
ideas extraordinary, but says understandingly that she does not
think she would be normal herself after five years at Downcroft.
She began to look me in the eye except when carried away by her own
odd ideas (usually she looks at one's aura overhead) and once, after
a particularly heavy snub from Mrs Strang, she stared for several
seconds mutely and I nearly slipped under the dining table. I began
to introduce a little conversation at meal-times just to keep them
apart, and things had grown so impossible that it was quite easy to
do - safe topics were the weather, crops, cows, and the newest
piglets.

I had my final uproar with Mrs Strang over the piglets. A new
girl, never having seen pigs, was given permission, by my special
request to Miss Palethorpe, to miss a few moments' housework to come
over to the farm and see them. Mrs Strang happened to overhear the
girl's delight later, was furious and punished her in spite of my
quiet protests, while Miss Palethorpe left me holding the baby as it
were, and later went off on her own leave without saying good-bye to
me. After the girls returned from mass home-leave in late August,
there was great unrest, abscondings, a little violence, and even a
day trip for the good girls failed miserably, with Mrs Strang

hinting that the cost of the trip had come from her own pocket –
'Thank you for your gratitude in return.'
   I don't propose to write any conclusions about Mrs Strang, except
that she seems unsuitable. She seems certain about whatever she
wants to believe, and there is often a grain of truth in what she
says, but it is somehow twisted and gross, though she frequently
accuses girls of twisting similarly and being two-faced. But if she
really felt right, she would have no need to be so frightened and to
cover herself against all eventualities. The whole place is fear-
ridden and Mrs Strang is the most frightened person of all. It
takes a long time to begin to see how fearful she is, because she
seems so much the opposite superficially, and is so frightening to
us too. But I think we sense without exactly knowing that she is
the most frightened, and this may be partly why we are sometimes
gentler and more protective of her than is justified when you think
of the girls.
   In writing to thank Mr French for his testimonial (which said I
'always kept the land in good heart') I added a second paragraph in
a final attempt to make my position clear:
      I very much regret leaving Downcroft. I imagine you will realize
      my real reason for leaving which is that I cannot agree with the
      present policy, although I tried to. Had I been more honest and
      less attached to the work, the girls and the whole place, I would
      have left much sooner than this. I only wish the girls could
      receive a glimmering of the enlightenment that Anna Herrison and
      I have found in our experience here – it must be wholly confusing
      to them.
Four of the committee came to see me on the farm to say good-bye,
half new members, as many who were almost friends are now ill or
dead. Recently I enjoyed a little brush with Mrs Percy who
irritates me since her speech on the need to k-e-e-p o-n
k-e-e-p-i-n-g o-n. Originally I seemed to have little choice over
the decision to keep battery hens as one of the four poultry systems
I run, but later the committee criticized the method (which I don't
like myself) and debated among themselves what to do. Mrs Percy
came to tell me their decision to scrap 90 cages and retain only 6
for 'teaching purposes'. I could not resist replying that the
battery-room is useful educationally, financially and occupation-
ally, and, if she was against it on principle as she said, why
should it ease her conscience to have six cages instead of 96? She
was taken aback, and they compromised by deciding to retain 32
cages. It annoyed me that the committee's eyes should seem only to
be open to the hens' questionable sufferings. The new arrangement
seemed extra tactless, as I found that the girls were identifying
each of the 32 birds with a girl in the school. Each bird has a
number and so has each girl on her clothes. Without saying
anything, I put some of the best new pullets into cages bearing the
numbers of some of the most downtrodden, despised girls in the
school, and Molly and June were delighted when they were the first
to start laying eggs.
   I have no illusions about the girls here. I know their
naughtiness like the back of my hand, but their other qualities
often give one fresh heart, and I do enjoy their warmth and humour
and liveliness and courage. Virtually all the girls have been a

tremendous help to me in my last weeks in a way I never expected. I
mind leaving excessively, but feel it essential to keep this hidden
because the girls would find it hard to understand that I am going
unwillingly and also, if colleagues or even Mrs Strang were to
sympathize suddenly, I could easily be in tears, and one can hardly
weaken when supposed to be leaving on principle! So, short of
hopping into an unprincipled battery cage, my days are numbered. It
is the girls who make my leaving tolerable in a surprising way.
Normally they are childish and grasping in their relationships, and
tend to be more so if staff are going. I dreaded having to try to
cope with this, as they do often want to drain the last drop of
sentimentality out of an unpleasant situation.

   But as it turns out I am just aware of real love and good-will
from most of them, though some of it appears in odd ways. (For
example, Kay, an ill-tempered girl, put her scrubbing brush in my
path as I was coming downstairs and said, 'Trip over that!' 'Why?'
'Because I don't want you to leave.' 'You'd rather I stayed with a
broken leg?' 'Yes.') For weeks beforehand they gave me small
presents such as book-marks, or combs, sheets of poetry and magazine
photos of animals, and very many little letters of good wishes for
the future, and I am keeping these. They did it very naturally, so
there is virtually no feeling of it being against the rules. Our
final good-byes are cheerful, with a strong impression that it has
been nice knowing each other, and that we can go on keeping in touch
after they are discharged, if they want to.

   On 3 September Highlight calved overnight and had milk fever but
recovered quickly with treatment. By 6 September everything on the
farm is in good order, and I have spent my last full day showing my
successor (who came yesterday and hardly spoke today) the routine.
I showed her the drains last of all to avoid saying good-bye to the
cows. When I compared her brawny forearm with mine at the tea-
table, it makes me wonder what our separate futures will hold.
Later in the evening I had done everything, so had a drink with
Paddy and Tommy.

I wasn't on duty on 7 September and left soon after breakfast. Miss
Siddy had a last minute request for thirty cracked eggs for the
house (she seems to think I will crack them on purpose, because
cracked ones are cheaper for her) and she was nearly in tears about
needing good wishes herself. I told Mrs Briggs I hoped her last
weeks would be as happy as possible - 'I don't much worry,' she
replied, 'the happiness is gone from Downcroft.' We all shook hands
with a variety of handshakes (Mrs Strang in her office in almost a
sad way) and, when it came to the point, after I had practised this
for months, I hardly noticed when I drove off down the front drive.

Jane Sparrow
31 May - 7 September 19X9

EPILOGUE

Now I am happily settled (and valued) as a social worker-cum-psychotherapist, and rarely experience difficulties at the same intensity as described above, partly because I know better how to meet (and by-pass) them.

As I feared in my final months at Downcroft, it was only afterwards that the impact of those five years really caught up with me - I was not actually ill, but physically and emotionally drained for some time. I was extremely fortunate in having a social work tutor who persevered in helping someone considered haunted-looking, tense, lacking in conversation, and overcontrolled in hiding feelings. In trying to ease my translation from farming, she asked my advice about the clipping of her yew hedge which, in an academic setting, caused me to consult a horticultural textbook, before clipping it therapeutically by the light of nature. It was suggested to me that I could perhaps continue as 'a weekend farmer'; however, the main attraction of farming for me lies in working alongside plants and animals while they develop daily of their own accord, and gradually I have found similar, even greater, satis-factions in plain social work.

Former Downcroft colleagues rallied to help eke out my small budget while I studied beforehand. (In my first term as 'a mature student', an external event occurred which I now regard as outrageous but which I took numbly in my stride at the time: my attendance was requested at a regional government department, apparently to ascertain (not very explicitly) whether I have Communist tendencies which might in future prove a contaminating influence. As I had no such leanings to declare, and nothing to conceal then except gross ignorance of politics in general, the interview was brief, vague, and ended on a friendly, informal note.)

It took several years subsequently, while establishing myself in truly satisfying work, before I could speak of Downcroft at any depth without trembling. One minor drawback was that initially I idealized social workers as standing for the complete opposite of all that was abhorrent in my first job, and therefore I have been slow in finding a new balance in exercising ordinary, benign authority (such as I did at Downcroft for the most part when less well qualified!) But it has been valuable to me personally to

127

re-live those early years of employment while editing the diary now,
and I feel more peaceful about it at last, though determined not to
rest until residential workers and inmates are treated with more
realistic respect. In so far as I am different in middle age from
my younger self, I am much less anxious to please, less keen to 'do
the right thing' at all costs, less afraid of other people's anger
and my own, more self-confident again (having lost confidence
straight after rather than during Downcroft days). In short, I have
largely overcome the social handicap of a very correct (though
affectionate and delightful) upbringing.

Never since have I encountered anybody else quite like Mrs
Strang, and though I might conceivably take on such a person as a
long-term patient in a rash moment, I would otherwise nowadays use a
longer spoon to sup with her, or preferably would sup in more
congenial company. One may sympathize with the Mrs Strangs of this
world without being drawn into their non-sense. She may or may not
still exist, in retirement, and would not recognize herself in these
pages, or alternatively would be certain, with a grain of truth,
that she once nourished a viper in her toughly vulnerable bosom.
Without doubt she wanted to be warm-hearted to me - it was I who
evaded a few inches of her complex apron-strings.

I am still in touch with many ex-Downcrofters, both with old
girls bringing up their own children and with ex-colleagues - that
is, with those who are still alive, and I assume those now dead are
resting in peace from their labours rather than 'bringing on
backward souls'. Dorcas works abroad with endless zeal, Romany
teaches now her children are launched, Alice married happily in late
middle age, Anna has made her name in more than one sphere of
interest - I am godmother to her eldest son, and she is coming to
stay with me for a weekend soon. Mr Marsh told me years later that
Anna's 'mantle' had fallen on to his shoulders after we left Glebe.
Tommy recently found strength to leave her post, Paddy will be
working hard somewhere unless she has burst a blood-vessel, Bill
Evans and Miss Gracey enjoy retirement. Those of us who are still
alive are all fairly all right now, though I am less sanguine about
the aftermath for the ex-Downcroft 'girls' I know.

Young social workers today seem more sturdy, less green, in
finding constructive ways of improving their working conditions, but
many remain uncertain how best to satisfy their requirements for
working well. I strongly endorse the idea that initial training
cannot in itself provide more than a foundation for meeting future
stress in the actual job. The main message in my diary is that
residential staff (as well as fieldworkers) must have a reliable
external person with whom they can discuss problems helpfully as
these happen. (If something does not happen, there is no need to
have stored textbook knowledge of it; if something unforeseen
happens, which it inevitably will, a half-forgotten textbook is not
enough.) And if we share Edith Cavell's hope to have a minimum of
hatred in our heart, in the realization that hatred and fear are
natural but destructive in our relationships with people who are not
easy to help, then we require a more responsive listener than a
four-legged pig on whom to off-load our discomfort (however
endearing and unchauvinistic real pigs may be).

In discussing the inevitable problems which arise in emotionally taxing work, the 'objective' rights and wrongs of colleagues in opposition to each other are fairly immaterial. There is no need for any superior, detached assessment as to whether Miss Gracey or Mrs Strang or Jane Sparrow is most realistic in her particular view of the current situation. What matters is that all workers as individuals should receive non-judgmental support towards overcoming the peculiar difficulties they personally experience within their job. Instead of having official standards laid down for them, residential staff need freedom 'to speak as they find' their own situation at the moment, in the hope that they will then live and work together in greater harmony.

I am much in two minds about publishing my private diary, so I would remind readers of what I implied at the beginning; truth is not only sometimes stranger than fiction but is unattainable by a fallible human being. Ultimately however, it is not a question of 'publish and be damned', but rather of requesting compassion for all the characters in my story. I wish to remain in quiet obscurity from now on, so these are my last words as an Old Downcroftonian:

To members of the uninitiated general public, may I say: if you read my diary with any amusement, read it also with sadness, and do not suppose yourselves much less corruptible under stress than the staff and girls I describe here. Try to imagine what residential life in general may be like, and extend your concern in practical ways (rather than withdraw in disgust over the occasional scandal which comes to light).

To current residents and ex-inmates of institutions of all kinds, I hardly know what to say, and can only hope my diary does not ring too true to you. Perhaps the main comfort lies in your realization that many of your staff find their chief satisfaction and enjoyment in their relationships with you. Often they enter this work because they want to be useful but, being as human as you are, they do not always achieve their aim as fully as they (and you) would wish. I hope you are free to discuss your own ideas with them about ways in which your situation together could be changed for the better.

To committee members, neo-inspectors, local authority administrators, and all senior officials with responsibility for Homes in which you are not yourselves resident: may I say plainly that you are a mixed blessing unless you so arrange things that residential staff are free to discuss their work problems on their own terms. Staff sometimes may feel constrained in trying to talk to you personally if they regard you as having influence over their joint career prospects, so you might need to employ an independent person with special skills. Surely this would be the cheapest way of ensuring that residents are reasonably well treated (assuming you learn to avoid selecting staff who are gross misfits in the first place). Also it is clear from my diary (and from general experience) that the Head may be unable to speak openly in the presence of junior staff, and vice versa; if you are trying to assist rather than to assess them, it will prove acceptable all round for both parties to discuss their work separately and confidentially. Certainly it takes courage on your part to risk 'knowing what is really going on' in residential institutions, but you will rarely discover serious problems through mere inspection, much less remedy the situation by keeping a watching brief from outside. However, if you employ the cheap safeguard of an independent visitor with special skills, you can afford to relax your vigilance, knowing that you have already taken the most effective precaution against mal-treatment and staff wastage.

To residential social workers and students, may I say that, unless you visualize continuing your work indefinitely in perfect comfort, you can best look after yourselves (and thereby care best for your fellow-residents, young and old) by making sure some appropriate person is available to look after your needs in extremely difficult work. Protest loudly if necessary in making your needs known.

Jane Sparrow